Christian Prayer

By W. ARNDT

PROFESSOR AT CONCORDIA SEMINARY
ST. LOUIS, MO.

ST. LOUIS, MO.
CONCORDIA PUBLISHING HOUSE
1937
PRINTED IN U. S. A.

DEDICATED TO THE MEMORY OF MY SAINTED WIFE

EMMA VETTER ARNDT

WHOSE LIFE, LONG-TIME SUFFERER THOUGH SHE
WAS, BEAUTIFULLY FLOWED IN THE CHANNELS OF
DEVOUT, CHRISTIAN PRAYER

FOREWORD

This essay originally was prepared for, and read at, the convention of the Oklahoma District of the Evangelical Lutheran Synod of Missouri, Ohio, and Other States held in Lahoma, Oklahoma, May, 1937. The request of the convention, addressed to Concordia Publishing House, to have the essay printed was acted on favorably by the Literature Board of the Evangelical Lutheran Synod of Missouri, Ohio, and Other States and by the Board of Directors of Concordia Publishing House. While I have endeavored to change the phraseology wherever the transfer of the discussion from the assembly floor to the printed page made this desirable or necessary, it may be that in a number of instances the manner of presentation still betrays the original purpose of the treatise. This stylistic imperfection will, I hope, be somewhat compensated for by the liveliness and directness which usually characterize the spoken message. I place this little volume into the hands of my readers with the reassuring invitation of the Savior: "Ask, and it shall be given you; seek, and ye shall find; knock, and it shall be opened unto you."   W. A.

TABLE OF CONTENTS

INTRODUCTION

In treating of prayer, we are dwelling on an intensely practical subject. We there speak not simply of something we *believe* — although our beliefs cannot and must not be excluded from the discussion — but of something we do. It is as practical a subject as we touch on when in our meetings we look each other straight in the eye and speak of Christian giving, Christian stewardship, attendance at divine services or business meetings, and the instruction of the young. Prayer, we all know, is an activity that Christians engage in, some more, some, alas! less. However we may define it, this aspect of it is undeniable. In other words, our subject takes us into the life that Christians lead and pertains to one of its most important functions. I hope everybody reading these words will make this a personal discussion for himself and, first and foremost, before he lets his mind make the round among his acquaintances and investigate and criticize their status as praying people, will have a good, penetrating look at his own condition and do such sweeping before his own door as the circumstances may require. Whenever a treatise on prayer is placed into our hands, an opportunity is afforded us to take an X-ray picture, as it were, of our own mental and spiritual inside, and we should not fail to make the photograph and to take the plate and to see where there is some dislocation or a menacing tumor or an atrophied organ. It is true that there is a doctrine or doctrines of prayer and that the whole subject can be dealt with in an abstract fashion, as a matter of theory. But I hope that no one of my readers will approach the discussion with such an intention. Rather let our state of mind be that of one of the disciples who, as Luke records, chap. 11, 1, said to Jesus, "Lord, teach us to pray." If we enter upon our study of Christian prayer in such a prayerful attitude, some good will be accomplished, and where the practise of prayer has been permitted to languish and almost disappear, it may, by the help of God, again be given a more prominent place in our thinking and in our life.

I

Praying is as universal as religion itself. To get a proper starting-point for this discussion, I am beginning with a statement of a very general nature. If one of us has been permitted to make a trip around the world and now gives an account of what

he has seen and heard, quite certainly he will allude to the many
shrines and temples which he observed wherever he went, places
of prayer, and to the many people he saw in the various countries
he visited who were in a praying attitude. That such scenes
greeted him in so-called Christian countries excites no great surprise. But it deserves special notice that non-Christian countries
do not form an exception in this respect. When our traveler
came to Constantinople, he saw the high towers of mosques, the
so-called minarets, and on them the public criers, the muezzins,
appearing at stated hours, five times a day, calling the people to
prayer, and he observed the faithful Mohammedans fall down on
their faces and in a devout fashion do homage to what they conceive to be the highest Being. In Jerusalem he saw Jews at the
so-called wailing-wall, supposed .to be a remnant of the old
walls of the city, and there weeping and praying. In darkest
Africa, when he visited villages of the Bushmen, he found these
benighted people praying to the Great Spirit. Arriving in India,
he was struck by the number of temples where prayers and sac-
rifices were offered. Soon he entered China, and again he saw
numerous temples, and many a person did he behold bowing
before some image and making requests.

The same kind of report can be made when a person, instead
of traveling around the world, makes a trip through history and
looks at the peoples of the globe in the various periods of their
existence. If we, with or without the Bible to aid us, trace the
manifold experiences, the joys and sorrows, of mankind as far
back as possible, immersing ourselves in the veritable ocean of
inscriptions, papyri, parchments, and tablets of various sorts that
learned and curious men have rescued out of the dust of the far-
distant past, one fact that stares us in the face at all times is that
the men of antiquity prayed.

There have been times, as we all know, when wicked individuals and groups made attempts to abolish religion and
prayer. It was tried, for instance, by the leaders of the French
Revolution toward the end of the eighteenth century, some of
whom urged that the King of heaven should be dethroned as
well as the kings here on earth. At first the populace of Paris
was wildly enthusiastic about this project. The services in the
churches of the city were suspended, and the guillotine was declared to have taken the place of the crucifix. But just as if
to show that man is incurably religious, a new cult was at once
introduced, which was called the worship of reason. A beautiful

young woman of unsavory reputation was taken to the chief church in Paris, Notre Dame, placed upon the altar, and there hailed as the representation of the Goddess of Reason. We see that the very people who looked upon religion as a superstition nevertheless could not quite relinquish all acts of worship. It was only about half a year later that Robespierre, who had now become the undisputed head of the republic, proposed to the convention that it adopt a decree the first paragraph of which was to read: "The French people recognize the existence of the Supreme Being and the immortality of the soul." This was adopted with exclamations of great joy, and the worship of reason was unceremoniously assigned to the junk-pile. A like fate, we may be sure, will befall the endeavors which are now being put forth with such fiendish, inhuman cruelty in Russia in opposition to all religious worship. That the present movement in Russia is dedicated to the principle that religion must be exterminated is stated in a recent article by one of the best-informed observers of conditions in Russia, P. E. T. Widdrington, writing in *Christendom* (January, 1937): "The Communist theory, to which the Soviet Government is committed, requires the liquidation of all churches and the destruction of the religious instinct." But he at once adds: "The exigencies of statecraft compelled the government to a recognition of the right of the Church to exist for the purposes 'of religious confession.'" The question whether there is any prospect of a larger measure of toleration he answers in the affirmative, and in giving reasons for this view he not only points to the political situation, which urges Russia to conciliate the United States and Great Britain, but especially to the lack of success which the Militant Atheists and the Godless Union have met with in their efforts to stamp out Christian worship. He quotes one of these atheistic propagandists as saying that not fewer than fifty million people in Russia have cut themselves off from religion, but he reminds us that Russia has 168,000,000 inhabitants and that according to these figures the vast majority of Russians has not yet disavowed belief in God and prayer. In brief, when on a day not far distant, if we read the signs of the times correctly, the last great crash will come and this universe will collapse, the divine Judge will not find many true believers, but He will, it is safe to predict, find some people engaging in what they call prayer. Praying will not die out.

In concluding this chapter, I cannot forbear quoting some eloquent words of Guizot, a famous French Protestant statesman and author of the nineteenth century, who in his book *The Church and Christian Society* wrote thus: "Alone of all beings here below, man prays! Among his moral instincts none is more natural, more universal, more indestructible, than prayer. The child inclines to it with eager docility; the old man betakes himself thither as to a refuge against decay and solitude. Prayer comes spontaneously to young lips, which with difficulty stammer out the name of God, and to dying lips, which no longer have strength to pronounce it. Among all nations, celebrated or obscure, civilized or barbarous, one meets at every step acts and forms of invocation. Wherever men live, in certain circumstances, at certain times, under the control of certain impressions of the soul, the eyes are raised, the hands clasp, the knees bend to implore aid or to render thanks, to adore or to appease. With transport or with fear, publicly or in the secrecy of his heart, it is to prayer that man betakes himself in the last resort, to fill up the void of his soul or to bear the burdens of his destiny; it is in prayer that he seeks, when all else fails, strength for his weakness, consolation in his grief, hope for his virtue." (Quoted by Patton, *Prayer and Its Remarkable Answers*, p. 117.)

II

This universality of prayer is due to man's inborn conviction that there is a supreme, almighty Being who has power to help or to destroy him and to whom he is responsible. That is the answer to the question so naturally asked by us, Why do all people, including, in cases of extreme peril, even many skeptics and scoffers, engage in prayer? However loud, blatant, and impersonating cock-sureness the atheists may be in proclaiming their negative "creed," the nations of the world, from the dawn of human history till today, have believed in the existence of a Supreme Being. The sophisticated unbelievers may, with an air of superiority, sneer at old Cicero's views, but the correctness of his assertion, pagan though he was, they cannot disprove, when he says: "No tribe is so barbarous, no one of all peoples so fierce, that the idea of God has not filled the mind. Many people hold depraved opinions about the gods, for this is a common thing, owing to corruption; all, however, believe that there is a divine power and essence. And indeed this is not brought about by a conference or agreement of men, this opinion is not confirmed by ordinances and by laws; but wherever there is a consensus of all nations, we must hold that we are dealing with a law of nature." (*Tusc. Disp.*, I.) When you consider, on the one hand, that God is invisible and that our scientists with all their microscopes and test tubes and telescopes and stratosphere expeditions can catch a glimpse of Him as little as we ordinary folk, with no expensive instruments and cloud-defying balloons to aid us, and that, on the other hand, all over the world mankind, except comparatively few individuals or small groups, hold and avow the firm belief that there is a God, we are confronted with a truly remarkable phenomenon. While there are many points on which the various nations of the earth do not agree; while, for instance, their ideas as to what is beautiful and valuable are by no means uniform; while their tastes and habits and rules of decorum and fashions and games are divergent enough to keep the inexperienced traveler in a constant state of excitement and anxiety, they all are convinced that there is a God who can hear prayers. A famous English scholar of our day, Gilbert Murray of Oxford, not at all a believer in God's revelation, says in one of his addresses: "We do seem to find, not only in all religions, but in practically all philosophies, some belief that man is not quite alone in the universe, but is met in his endeavors toward the good by some external help or sympathy. We find it everywhere in the unsophisticated man. We find it in the unguarded self-revelations of the most severe and conscientious atheists." And at the conclusion of his address, after having thrown doubt on the validity of this universal conviction, he has this final remark: "It is a belief very difficult to get rid of." (The Stoic philosophy.) So it is that people pray, and when they do not know to whom precisely the prayer should be addressed, they erect an altar and inscribe on it "To the unknown God." It all confirms the truth of what Paul and Barnabas proclaimed of the living God, "He left not Himself without witness," Acts 14, 17.

III

Not everything that bears the name is a really God-pleasing prayer. When we say this, we draw attention to an obvious truth, which, however, is frequently ignored by our superficial age, governed as it is more by mere attractive appearances and weak sentimentalities than a robust sense of reality and truth. We are all agreed that this is a world which abounds in sham and deceit; we have a Pure Food and Drug Act to prevent the public from being duped by manufacturers who would like to fill bottles with slightly colored *aqua pura* and then sell it as the most recently discovered infallible remedy for coughs, rheumatism, and lumbago; there are legal ways of keeping a dairy concern which depends more on the water-pump than on its cows for its output from carrying on its hydraulic business. But when we come to praying, many people act as if in their opinion the mere label suffices. The colossal swindle which numerous heathen Chinese are not ashamed to practise on their divinities when they, to appease them in a certain situation, bring an offering of, let us say, one hundred thousand dollars in paper money, which they, with a religious air, burn as a sacrifice, but which is merely fake money, bought in the store around the corner at so much an ounce, is, one regrets to say it, duplicated rather often in Christian countries through the many idle prayers that are spoken on the most diverse occasions. The question, What constitutes a true and what a false prayer? is not before us as yet. Here I merely wish to state that we must not be content with the appellation prayer, since often the name and the reality are divorced. That we are here dealing with Scripture teaching is indicated to us by several episodes in the Sacred Record. There is the case of Saul, who, as we are told, inquired of the Lord, that is, after a fashion prayed to God, but whom the Lord did not answer, neither by dream nor by Urim nor by prophets, 1 Sam. 28, 6. Likewise is it evident from the case of the prophets of Baal, who in their encounter with Elijah cried from morning even till noon, "O Baal, hear us!" but in response to whose crying, as the holy writer informs us, there was no voice nor any that answered, 1 Kings 18, 26. The sacred narrative continues in most dramatic fashion: "It came to pass at noon that Elijah mocked them and said, Cry aloud, for he is a god; either he is talking, or he is pursuing, or he is in a journey, or peradventure he sleepeth and must be awaked. And they cried aloud and cut themselves after their manner with knives and lancets till the blood gushed out upon them. And it came to pass when midday was passed and they prophesied till the time of the offering of the evening sacrifice, that there was neither voice nor any to answer nor any that regarded." What these people called praying evidently was no praying at all. Of the numerous passages where God directly condemns certain "prayers" I shall merely quote two. One is taken from the New Testament, Jas. 4, 3: "Ye ask and receive not because ye ask amiss that ye may consume it upon your lusts."

Note the words "ye ask amiss"; your praying is wrong; it is not acceptable to God. The other passage is taken from the Old Testament, Prov. 1, 24—29: "Because I have called and ye refused; I have stretched out My hand and no man regarded, but ye have set at naught all My counsel and would none of My reproof, I also will laugh at your calamity, I will mock when your fear cometh; when your fear cometh as desolation and your destruction cometh as a whirlwind; when distress and anguish cometh upon you. Then shall they call upon Me, but I will not answer; they shall seek Me early, but they shall not find Me for that they hated knowledge and did not choose the fear of the Lord." These are devastating words, showing that we have to distinguish between prayers and prayers. It must always be a matter of grave concern to us that our prayers do not partake of the nature of wax roses, which to the superficial observer look fresh and beautiful, but in reality lack all life and fragrance.

IV

Prayer is a religious act, consisting in speaking to God. So we might frame a very simple definition of prayer. For the present we simply wish to emphasize that the act performed in prayer is speaking, speaking to somebody different from ourselves. That we are here dealing with a religious rite is obvious, is universally acknowledged, and requires no special elucidation. The other point asserted — that it is a speaking — will not be disputed either. "When ye pray, say," so Jesus begins His instruction as He teaches His disciples the Lord's Prayer, Luke 11, 2. That the speaking does not have to be done in an audible way we are all agreed, I am sure, particularly when we consider that the praying of our deaf-and-dumb fellow-Christians by the use of the sign-language is certainly true praying even though not one word is heard during the whole prayer. Speaking is communicating one's thoughts to somebody else. When Helen Keller spells out her words on your hand, employing the sense of touch, she is truly speaking to you. This will remind us that praying can be done by means of our thoughts, since thus we can communicate our sentiments to God; He, as Scripture says, understands our thoughts afar off.

Here let us fix on the practical importance of the truth we are considering. If prayer is speaking, then we cannot perform it by putting a beautifully bound prayer-book which our pastor has ordered from Concordia Publishing House or a similar firm on the table of our living-room, thinking that now we can say with a sigh of relief, Here is another duty, the duty of praying, properly and handsomely fulfilled. Purchasing a prayer-book and domiciling it in the most respectable and conspicuous spot of our home is not yet Christian prayer. Again, when we attend a service in our church and the pastor leads the congregation in prayer and we have risen with the brethren' and have adopted, as we should, a reverential attitude, but let our mind wander about in the universe and calculate how large a profit the rise in cattle prices, reported to us by our neighbor just before the service, will mean in our particular case, and with a growing feeling of comfort we contemplate how our bank account will swell, we are not praying. Whatever the pastor and the others in the church may be doing, we are not speaking, that is, communicating our thoughts, to somebody else.

Some people have the entertaining habit of speaking to themselves, at times quite audibly, and it is surprising how fast the hours flit by for them while they are thus pleasantly occupied. What they all say to themselves in an afternoon would probably fill the pages of a moderately sized newspaper. Now, such communing with oneself, wholesome and necessary as it often is, is not prayer, because prayer is speaking to somebody distinct from oneself, to God. How earnestly we should admonish each other and our own selves that instead of engaging in dialogs with our own ego, which at times are entirely vain, we ought to commune with our God, speak to Him, pour out our hearts in His presence. For the nonce let us fix this thought firmly in our mind: Prayer is an activity consisting in this, that we speak, speak to God.

V

That it is God to whom we speak in prayer requires special emphasis. When we say that our prayers must be addressed to God, we voice a truth which every Christian rightly regards as obvious. Who else than God could be addressed in prayer? Everybody admits that prayer is intended to put us in contact with that unseen Person and Power, who is so far and yet so near, of whom Tennyson has said:

Speak to Him, thou, for He heareth,
And Spirit with spirit may meet;
Closer is He than breathing
And nearer than hands and feet.

Should we call on the sun or the moon or one of the stars or on the ceaselessly moving, murmuring ocean? They cannot hear us. Or shall we speak to the storm as with lightning and thunder in terrible swiftness it rushes through the land, dealing out destruction where it passes? It cannot comprehend one word we say. Or shall we address our prayers to some of the grand heroes and leaders of the past, such as prophets and apostles, or kings, generals, and statesmen, who with wisdom, energy, and valor worked to make this world a better place to live in? They have left us, and praying to them would be a futile gesture, an idle, useless ceremony. But now listen to what our sacred Book says of God, for instance, in the incomparably majestic words of Ps. 139: "O Lord, Thou hast searched me and known me. Thou knowest my downsitting and mine uprising; Thou understandest my thought afar off. Thou compassest my path and my lying down and art acquainted with all my ways. For there is not a word in my tongue but, lo, O Lord, Thou knowest it altogether. Thou hast beset me behind and before and laid Thine hand upon me. Such knowledge is too wonderful for me; it is high, I cannot attain unto it. Whither shall I go from Thy Spirit, or whither shall I flee from Thy presence? If I ascend up into heaven, Thou art there; if I make my bed in hell, behold, Thou art there. If I take the wings of the morning and dwell in the uttermost parts of the sea, even there shall Thy hand lead me, and Thy right hand shall hold me," vv. 1—10. With what poetic grandeur and convincing clearness is the truth brought out here that God can hear us when we pray, regardless of apparent difficulties caused by tremendous distances or by the seemingly impenetrable secrecy which envelops the unexpressed and inarticulate sighs and moans of our heart! Therefore, if prayer is really to be prayer, it must be addressed to God. He is the only One who possesses the qualities of omnipresence and omniscience, which enable Him to hear even the faintest utterance of our soul.

Again, does not the Bible in its sixty-six books show us with overwhelming force and directness that our prayers must be spoken to God? He is the One to whom the children of God mentioned in the Scriptures went with their prayers and petitions, whether it was an old patriarch like Abraham, who pleaded with God for his son Ishmael, or the writer of the last book of the New Testament, St. John, who in Rev. 15 reports this heavenly prayer: "Great and marvelous are Thy works, Lord God Almighty; just and true are Thy works, Thou King of saints. Who shall not fear Thee, O Lord, and glorify Thy name? For Thou only art holy; for all nations shall come and worship before Thee; for Thy judgments are made manifest." Besides these examples we have definite commands in the Scriptures ordering us to go to God with our prayers, such as 1 Chron. 16, 11: "Seek the Lord and His strength; seek His face continually." Indeed, if my readers and I were to look at all the passages which directly or by implication instruct us to address our prayers to God, the size of this book would have to be increased enormously.

There is a practical consideration here which presses its claims upon us. If prayer means communing with God, it is something that must fill us with solemn awe. As little as we may speak *of* God without feelings of absolute reverence and humility, being aware of the incalculable gap existing between Him and us, so little may we engage in conversation *with* God in prayer, which takes us into the divine presence, without a deeply felt conviction that we are treading on holy ground, as it were, and that all levity, frivolity, indifference, and thoughtlessness must be avoided. When we speak to our superiors here on earth, we know it is proper that the swaggering air which perhaps we are fond of be abandoned and respect and decorum be exhibited. How much more should we realize that, when we approach the great Ruler of heaven and earth, we should be conscious of the importance of the occasion and not speak to Him as if we carried on a conversation with an equal. Let us not forget that the same Scriptures which picture God as love speak of Him as a "consuming fire."

VI

Prayers not addressed to the true God are no prayers at all. My readers will probably say that all that we have dwelt on in the foregoing section is so perfectly patent and well known to every Bible-reader that it seems strange any one would consider it to require special emphasis. That is correct; but what makes it imperative that we do not slight this truth in our instruction, regarding it as too self-evident, is that it is denied, and objected to, by many people.

There are men who hold that the identity of the Being you pray to is of little consequence, but that what counts and gives prayer its dignity, worth, and efficacy is sincerity and earnestness as you voice your petitions. These people will say that you, in speaking your prayers, will of course have to entertain the honest belief that you are addressing the Deity, that, however, if you should be in error as to that point, your prayer will not suffer and lose its value. It is an idea which Lessing somewhat sponsored in his celebrated drama *Nathan der Weise,* in which the fundamental thought is that the true religion cannot be discovered any more, yet that this does not make much difference either as long as the devotees of Judaism, Mohammedanism, and Christianity manifest love towards each other and cease vilifying and persecuting their opponents. It is a belief that dictated those infamous lines which reflected, and still reflect, the views of many rationalists:

Wir glauben all' an *einen* Gott,
Christ, Jude, Tuerk' und Hottentott.
(To one god render honor due
Turk, Christian, Hottentot, and Jew.)

If we analyze what lies at the basis of this view, we shall see that it is the opinion that, no matter to whom our prayers are addressed, ultimately the Supreme Being in whom the various nations believe is one and the same and all prayers that are uttered in sincerity and devotion are acceptable to Him.

This is one of the foundation-stones in the system of Freemasonry, the mother of lodgery. Freemasonry, as we know, insists that all who become members of its order must believe in a Supreme Being; but whether that Supreme Being is Allah, the god of the Mohammedans, or the antichristian god of the Jews, or the Triune God whom we adore, or some pagan deity, is unessential according to its tenets. Those who have entered the order on this basis, regardless of how they conceive of the Supreme Being, all join in prayer; and it is held that these variously addressed utterances are all God-pleasing and worthy of the name prayer. We therefore find that in the halls of this lodge Jews, Turks, Christians, and possibly others may be seen singing this stanza of a funeral ode, printed by Mackey in his *Masonic Ritualist:*

O Lord of all, below, above,
Fill our hearts with truth and love;
When dissolves our earthly tie,
Take us to the lodge on high.

We must remember that Freemasonry by no means wishes to foster belief in the Triune God, the Father of our Lord Jesus Christ, but merely demands of those who are candidates for admission that they avow belief in the existence of a Supreme Being and then direct prayers to this Being, whoever he may be in the opinion of the individual members. That Freemasonry started in the soil of what is called deism, the view that belief in the existence and supremacy of a god is all that has to be held on the subject of the Deity and that acceptance of the revelation of God in the Bible is by no means necessary, seems an undisputed fact. It has been correctly pointed out that such a course does not mean that one is neutral on the question Who is the true God? but that one creates a false god, a deity opposed to the God of the Scriptures, Father, Son, and Holy Ghost.

One of the prominent characteristics of what we call Modernism, the religion which terms itself Christian, but discards whatever in the Bible it cannot understand or what apparently is contradicted by modern science, is this very view, that it does not make much or any difference what God you believe in or to whom our prayers are spoken as long as you are sincere in your beliefs and are imbued with the spirit of love for your fellow-men. One of the spokesmen of Modernism, Wm. A. Vrooman, in his book entitled *Progressive Christianity* (p. 138), says: "We may also venture to say that this perception of the way to the highest human life has not been confined to those who accept the Christian traditions. As an interpreter of the philosophy of India a great Hindu scholar declares: 'If we want to escape from sin, we must escape from selfishness, and we should realize in our life and conduct that all things are in God and of God. . . . Moral life is a God-centered life, a life of patient love and enthusiasm for humanity, of seeking the infinite through the finite, and not a mere selfish adventure for small ends.' Who shall say that men having this faith need be excluded from the fellowship with Christ, and those who follow Him, because they lack the traditional Christian doctrines?" So Vrooman is willing to let this Hindu be in his religious fellowship, which implies that he would regard his prayers as genuine and as truly pleasing to God. All who know something about Modernism will at once say that the view Vrooman voices is consistent with the general position of the Modernists, who have adopted as one of the chief planks in their platform the declaration that religion is not a matter of beliefs but of life and that what we want is not creeds but deeds. We can all see that the logical outcome of such a view is the assumption that all prayers are satisfactory if they are earnest, representing genuine, honest convictions, and have as their background a moral life.

Is it necessary, after what has been stated in the preceding chapter, to present a long refutation of this position? That our God, being omniscient, is aware of all the petitions uttered, of all the cries of agony sent forth, of all the secret sighs and lamentations of agitated human hearts on the face of our globe, whether the petitioners and suffering ones be Christians or not, we know very well. But His being aware of these utterances does not make them true prayers. Praying, as we said above, is speaking to God, the true God, Father, Son, and Holy Spirit. If one speaks but does not speak to Him, can that justly be called a prayer? Probably somebody will say, It is true, in strict logic such prayers are not real prayers. But since God knows of all requests, whether addressed to Him or not, He will *consider* them true prayers. We know that He is kind and good toward all creatures, the rational and the irrational, and hence He will accept their prayers as if they were proper and genuine. In reply we have to say that certainly it is not for us to decide a question of this nature, but for God Himself. Whether we can say anything positive on it will depend on whether God has given us a revelation on this topic. And we must say that He has given us such a revelation. Think of the description He has given us of the attempts of the priests of Baal from which I quoted before, where we are shown how these priests tried to arouse their god and induce him to intervene in their behalf. We have no reason to doubt their sincerity; and the vehemence and energy in their attempts at prayer they amply attested by not only leaping and shouting, but cutting themselves with knives and lancets. But not a flicker of recognition did God grant them. On the contrary, His prophet Elijah heaped ridicule and contempt on their wild, noisy demonstrations; and finally God, by sending fire on the sacrifice of Elijah but not on theirs, completely disavowed them.

We all know the words of Jesus spoken to Satan: "It is written, Thou shalt worship the Lord, thy God, and Him only shalt thou serve." Prayer, it cannot be denied, comes under the head of worship. God, then, expressly forbids that prayer be offered to anybody but Himself. Similarly He says in Is. 42, 8: "I am the Lord, that is My name; and My glory will I not give to another, neither My praise to graven images." It is a part of the glory of God that people call on Him in prayer and thanksgiving. We see, then, that He definitely tells us that this glory He will not share with anybody else. It is in language which makes us tremble in our innermost being that He says in giving the Ten Commandments, after He has told His people to have no other gods before Him: "I, the Lord, thy God, am a jealous God." Let us not think that He is a weak, indulgent Father like so many human fathers nowadays, who pay the bills of their children and let them do as they please. No, He is a jealous God, insisting that His authority be recognized and that His sovereignty be not assigned to somebody else.

But the good intentions, somebody will say, the good intentions! Surely God will not disregard the good intentions of the Mohammedans and heathen and Jews when they in pain and anguish send up prayers to their fictitious deities. The good intentions! Intentions are of tremendous importance; but how little can they make a wrong course right! The physician has the good intention of helping his patient, but if he through some mistake hands him deadly poison instead of the proper remedy and the patient dies, the good intention will not bring the latter back to life. Peter had the good intention of advancing his Master's welfare, and hence, when the Savior had spoken of His coming suffering, the apostle took Him and began to rebuke Him, saying, "Be it far from Thee, Lord; this shall not be unto Thee." Yes, Peter's intentions were good, but he received the severest and most withering rebuke that any of the disciples of Jesus ever had to hear from the lips of the Savior, "Get thee behind Me, Satan; thou art an offense to Me; for thou savorest not the things that be of God, but those that be of men," Matt. 16, 23. Hence let us not assume that good intentions will give to an utterance addressed to a false god the status of a true prayer unless God says so. And such a declaration He has not given us. It is with a heart full of pity and sympathy that we think of the heathen, who in their blindness are muttering prayers before idols, and of all the Jews and Mohammedans and all the deists in the lodges and elsewhere, who offer up their petitions to a fictitious ruler of the universe. But such feelings of pity cannot blind us to the fact that, since these people are not praying to the true God, their praying is futile and vain. It will not help them that one calls that which is black white or that which is crooked straight, in other words, that one tries to justify their prayers by all sorts of sophistries and superingenious arguments. But what we ought to do if we are genuinely concerned about their welfare is to bring them a knowledge of the truth and to enlighten them on who the true God is and what constitutes genuine prayer. Not far-fetched speculations as to the possible value their so-called prayers may have, but earnest mission-work is what is needed.

VII

To be truly Christian and acceptable, a prayer must be spoken in the name of Jesus. This assertion rests not on any fine-spun speculations of our own fancy but on definite words of Jesus, spoken in the night in which He was betrayed, when He was lovingly bidding His disciples farewell and comforting them with respect to His impending death. These words springing up from the deep fountain of eternal mercy, when the shadow of the cross had become terribly distinct, are very precious to us, and with gratitude we contemplate them. John 14, 13 f.: "Whatsoever ye shall ask in My name, that will I do, that the Father may be glorified in the Son. If ye shall ask anything in My name, I will do it." John 15, 16: "Ye have not chosen Me, but I have chosen you and ordained you that ye should go and bring forth fruit and that your fruit should remain, that whatsoever ye shall ask of the Father in My name, He may give it you." John 16, 23 f.: "And in that day shall ye ask Me nothing. Verily, verily, I say unto you, Whatsoever ye shall ask the Father in My name, He will give it you. Hitherto have ye asked nothing in My name; ask, and ye shall receive that your joy may be full." John 16, 26 f.: "At that day ye shall ask in My name; and I say not unto you that I will pray the Father for you, for the Father Himself loveth you because ye have loved Me and have believed that I came out from God." It is very evident that here the followers of Jesus are instructed to voice their petitions in His name and that great promises are attached to such prayers. What does the phrase mean? Somebody might think that what is enjoined thereby is that you have to mention the name of Jesus in your prayer and that such mention is the magic key which opens the treasure-house of God to the petitioners and permits them to take what they please. That such an opinion would be wrong we see at once from the model prayer which Jesus has taught us. The name of Jesus does not occur in it, which is quite convincing proof that a prayer, to be proper and acceptable, does not necessarily have to contain the name of Jesus. Certainly we like to mention the name of our blessed Savior when we speak to God, and we often conclude our petitions by saying, "This we ask in the name of Jesus." Every Christian will have to admit that such phraseology is beautiful and to be commended. But what needs to be said here is that these words are not essential and that a prayer may be uttered in the name of Jesus without employment of that particular phrase. While we gladly join this phrase to our prayer to remind ourselves that our petitions must be spoken in the name of our heavenly Lord, the question presents itself as one ponders the subject a little more whether merely the insertion of the words "This we ask in the name of Jesus" actually in every case makes the prayer one that is truly spoken in the name of our divine Master — a question which, we must sadly admit, is to be answered in the negative.

If, then, it must be granted that not the employment of a particular phrase is here to be thought of, what is it that the Savior may have in mind when giving this instruction? The meaning is quite simple: Coming before God, we should have the name of Jesus upon us and exhibit it, as it were. The Savior tells us that we should appear before God as His disciples, His followers. "In His name" is here equivalent to "with His name." It means that we plead the merits of Christ as we voice our supplications, pointing to His atonement as the basis of our assurance that we shall be heard. It means that we hide the filthy rags of our sins and imperfections under Jesus' blood and righteousness and make these treasures our beauty and glorious dress as we approach Jehovah's awful throne. If our petition concludes: "Hear us, O great God, not for the sake of our own worthiness, but for the sake of what Thy Son hath accomplished as our Substitute," and this is our true sentiment, then we pray in the name of Jesus. What is essential, according to this conception of the phrase, is not that the name of Jesus be spoken or His work be referred to in definite words, but that a person come before God as a true believer in Christ, having erected the cross of Calvary in his heart, relying on Jesus' vicarious sacrifice. Undoubtedly many a prayer is truly spoken in the name of Jesus when it consists of nothing but the sigh "O God, help me," because the person praying is in all simplicity basing his trust on the work of the God-man.

If anybody should doubt that we are here correctly interpreting the expression "prayer in the name of Jesus," let him carefully consider the connection in which these words occur in John 14, 12—14: "Verily, verily, I say unto you, He that believeth on Me, the works that I do shall he do also; and greater works than these shall he do because I go unto My Father. And whatsoever ye shall ask in My name, that will I do that the Father may be glorified in the Son. If ye ask anything in My name, I will do it." You observe that Christ is speaking of people that believe on Him. Such people, He says, will do the works that Christ Himself does, even greater ones (referring undoubtedly to the extension of the Church through the preaching of the Gospel). And then He speaks of prayer in His name. It evidently is a prayer which is offered by persons who come before God as devout followers of His Son. If we say to God, "Heavenly Father, we are praying as disciples of Jesus," that is praying in the name of Jesus. So we may rest assured that we have correctly apprehended the meaning of this phrase.

Luther has some comments on this matter, which, as usually, go to the very core of the subject. With respect to John 16, 23 he says: "The third point in this text is the expression 'in My name,' which is the main thing and the foundation on which faith is to rest and from which it receives its value and dignity so as to be acceptable to God and its force and power that it must be heard. And this frees us from all heavy anxiety and useless worry (which most of all keeps us from praying and makes us faint-hearted), the worry about our worthiness, that we are not to inquire nor be concerned about it, but disregard both worthiness and unworthiness and base our prayer on Him and pray in His name." And then Luther paraphrases the words of the Savior thus: "My beloved, let your situation be what it pleases; if you cannot pray by yourself and in your own name (a thing which you are not to do), then pray in My name; if you are not sufficiently worthy and holy, let Me have these qualifications; trust in Me and My name and say, Dear Lord, I must and will pray according to Thy command and promise; if I cannot do it well, and if it lacks value and power, in my name, then let it have validity and excellence in the name of Christ, my Lord."

Now let us note some of the truths which are implied in the teaching we have just considered. If all prayer must be spoken in the name of Jesus, then no one except true Christians can really offer up acceptable prayers to God. The Jew, who rejects Christ as the Messiah and Jehovah; the Mohammedan, who sees in Him nothing but a great prophet; the Unitarian, who refuses to accept Jesus as his Lord and God; the heathen, who has not heard of Christ at all or, if he has heard of Him, turns away from Him in scorn to worship his idols; the skeptic, who doubts almost everything and is not quite sure of his own existence, much less of that of Jesus of Nazareth, all these, since they do not believe in Christ and come before God as His disciples, do not utter true Christian prayers. We see that the prayers of the deistic lodges, which often are couched in phraseology as gorgeous as the uniforms of the Shriners, are no prayers at all, for they are not spoken in the name of Jesus. But is it not to be feared, too, that many congregation-members who in their churches join in beautiful prayers which clearly express belief in Christ or who use handsome prayer-books that have the cross not only on the outside cover, but exalt it duly in the various sections, are not speaking true prayers because in their hearts they trust in their own merits and good deeds and hence are not praying in the name of Jesus? It is not our position before a gilded crucifix or the purchase for our bedroom of an "Ecce Homo" picture of Christ, much as we ought to prize it, or the wearing of the little gold cross in our coat lapel, though we rightly encourage such a testimony of our heart's allegiance, — I say, nothing of such an outward nature betokening that we honor Christ really gives to our prayers this quality or attribute that it can be said to be spoken in the name of Jesus. What gives it this essential requisite is true, living faith in Christ as our Redeemer, so simple and yet altogether unattainable through our own reason and strength, a possession frequently of babes and sucklings and yet often not found with the learned and the mighty; faith which appropriates all that Christ has lived and died for, makes the beggar incalculably rich, and gives the weary and the heavy-laden sweet rest and that peace which the world does not know. Hold this faith as a living reality, approach God as one who is filled with this faith, and then, whether you make special mention of Christ or not, your prayer will be spoken in the name of Jesus. It ought to be pointed out that also the Lord's Prayer, in order to be God-pleasing, must be spoken in this fashion.

VIII

The contents of our prayers may be described as petitions and thanksgiving. In this proposition we are touching on a phase of our subject to which we need devote but a modicum of time, because what is to be said on it is quite patent. In one of the preceding chapters we saw that prayer consists in speaking to

God, a definition which is borne out, for instance, by Ps. 27, 8: "When Thou saidst, Seek ye My face, my heart said unto Thee, Thy face, Lord, will I seek"; for seeking the face of God means as much as communing with Him, speaking to Him. But the question arises, What is it that we shall say to Him in these communings? That we, standing before His divine majesty, must not utter the chafflike drivel, the inane platitudes which constitute the bulk of ordinary conversation, is clear at once. What, then, are we to say? The Bible has many hints for us on that head. We can, however, put all our prayers into two classes, that of petitions and that of thanksgiving. When St. Paul says 1 Tim. 2, 1: "I exhort therefore that, first of all, supplications, prayers, intercessions, and giving of thanks be made for all men," he uses four terms to describe the speaking to God in which we should engage; but if you look at them closely, you will see that they easily fall into the two classes mentioned. Supplication is a term for beseeching, entreating, denoting our asking for something; prayer is simply the general designation for communion with God; the word translated "intercession" signifies, strictly speaking, according to the Greek, interview and petition. So we see that the first three terms in Paul's instruction all describe either speaking to God in general or what we call petition. And beside them the apostle places the giving of thanks.

Confession of sins has been mentioned as another topic of our communion with God, and we know that in the Bible, especially in the great prayer-book of the Bible, the Psalms, such confession occupies a prominent place. But it hardly requires a category of its own, because it naturally falls into the class of petitions; for when we confess our sins, there is always connected with it the prayer for forgiveness. At times it is thought that adoration should be given a special class. Every Bible-reader is aware that in the prayers of the Scriptures this aspect of communion with God occupies a prominent place. "Lord, Thou hast been our Dwelling-place in all generations" (Ps. 90, 1); "The Lord is in His holy temple, let all the earth keep silence before Him" (Hab. 2, 20); "O Lord, how great are Thy works, and Thy thoughts are very deep" (Ps. 92, 5): these passages ring out like silver bells on a quiet Sunday morning, calling on all men to worship our great God. But it is very evident that they can well be put under the head of thanksgiving. That intercession in behalf of our fellow-men must be one of the things we bring before God we shall all readily acknowledge. But intercession does not require a special division, for it is simply a part of our petitions. In concluding this merely formal chapter, let me say that Luther is right when he says (X, 2204): "There are only two ways of dealing with God, namely, by thanksgiving and petition."

IX

Every Christian prays. That is the very definite assertion of Luther, who, in commenting on John 14, 13. 14, writes: "You can find no Christian without prayer, just as little as a living human being without a pulse; for this is never inactive, but moves and beats in its own way, although a person sleeps or does something else and is not aware of it." (VIII, 363.) And in another passage he says: "Just as a cobbler makes a shoe and a tailor a coat, so a Christian has to pray. His business is to pray." (Walch, XXII, 807.)

If we look into the Scriptures, we shall find that the great Reformer did not exaggerate or permit his fancy to make unwarranted flights when he described prayer as a universal Christian activity. Think of the great chapter in the middle of the Epistle of St. Paul to the Romans, chap. 8. One truth which the apostle there triumphantly asserts is that the Holy Spirit dwells in the Christian and makes him cry, "Abba, Father." And in that connection you have the comforting declaration: "Likewise the Spirit also helps our infirmities; for we know not what we should pray for as we ought, but the Spirit itself maketh intercession for us with groanings which cannot be uttered." Hence, as certain as it is that the Holy Spirit dwells in Christians, so certain it is that they pray. This is confirmed in Gal. 4, 5: "And because ye are sons, God hath sent forth the Spirit of His Son into your hearts crying, Abba, Father."

Accordingly we find that the children of God whose portraits are drawn for us in the Scriptures were people of prayer. Of the old patriarchs Abraham, Isaac, and Jacob we read that they called upon God and built altars at which they worshiped. Of Moses it is not only recorded again and again that he cried to the Lord, but from his heart and mouth and pen has come one of the most beautiful and touching prayers in the Bible, Ps. 90. That David was a man of frequent and devout prayer we know from the Book of Psalms, many of which the shepherd-king himself composed, sang, and prayed. A very consecrated, God-fearing king of

Judah was Hezekiah, and in the Scriptures several prayers which he spoke have been handed down to us. In the New Testament we find the first Christian congregation continuing steadfast in the apostles' doctrine and fellowship and in breaking of bread and in prayers. Consider the case of the greatest one of the apostles, a giant among his contemporaries, many of whom were of more than ordinary spiritual stature, Paul. Christ had appeared to him before Damascus, and, blinded by the brightness of the heavenly vision, he was sitting in a house in Damascus, neither eating nor drinking. What was he doing? Christ, speaking to Ananias, whom He was sending to Paul, said about the latter in words of deep pathos, "Behold, he prayeth." Yes, the former persecutor was now praying. And what a life of prayer it is that he now begins according to the testimony of the Book of Acts and his own epistles! An English scholar, after drawing attention to the short prayers of Paul, consisting of exclamations or of brief sentences of invocation, benediction, or thanksgiving, has listed thirteen special kinds of prayer found in Paul's letters: prayers for the abounding of charity; for entire sanctification; for the good pleasure of God; for everlasting consolation; for love and patience; for corporate perfection; for unity of believers; for hope; for knowledge of God's will; for full assurance of knowledge; for the glory of the inheritance; for the indwelling of the Trinity; for perseverance to the day of Christ. (W. B. Pope, *Taking Hold of God*, quoted by Zwemer, p. 140.) The seer St. John, in concluding the book which is the last one in our New Testament, breathes the prayer which has ever since been reechoing in Christian hearts, "Even so, come, Lord Jesus." What a galaxy of saints that prayed the Bible places into its firmament for us to behold, substantiating that wherever there is true Christianity there is prayer.

These last words may seem like a hard saying to one or the other of us who has become rather indolent in prayer and has almost reached the point that he will pray only when he has to, being compelled by the proprieties of the occasion, whose heart has been drawing away farther and farther from the heavenly Father, and whose messages to heaven have become about as rare as rainfall in Egypt. If there is such a one among my readers, let him see that, as his prayers become less and less frequent, his spiritual life is losing in quantity and quality and that soon the hour may come when the all-seeing eye of God will pronounce him spiritually dead and angels will weep over his demise. Let everybody who has become indifferent in regard to this matter see that his slothfulness is due to the influence of his evil nature, the Old Adam, who secretly strives to overcome the power of the Holy Spirit in us, who is a Spirit of prayer.

X

Prayer is a part not of justification, but of sanctification. In saying that prayer is a part not of justification, but of sanctification, we are in a way summarizing some of the truths which were pointed to before. It is one way of bringing out sharply that we do not become Christians through prayer, but that prayer presupposes our having accepted Christ as our Savior, in other words, that only a Christian can pray. To us members of the Lutheran Church, God in His mercy has given the special grace that we carefully differentiate between justification and sanctification. It is a part of our spiritual heritage, which we are exceedingly careful to keep unimpaired, knowing how easily an error here will vitiate the whole system of doctrine. We are mindful, too, of the important role which the doctrine of justification played in the reformation of the Church, when Luther, acting the part of youthful David, defeated the giant Goliath, whose headquarters are at the Vatican in Rome. That smooth stone from the brook which, sped on its way by Luther's sling, decided the battle was the doctrine of justification by grace, through faith. This being our conviction, it is but natural that, when we speak of something pertaining to Christian faith and life we should ask ourselves whether it belongs to justification or sanctification and that we now raise this question touching Christian prayer.

Now, that prayer is not a part of justification is evident from this, that all works we do are rigorously excluded from justification; and prayer is a work of ours. "Therefore we conclude that a man is justified by faith, without the deeds of the Law," says the Apostle Paul in one of his well-known positive declarations, Rom. 3, 28. And again he says: "Knowing that a man is not justified by the works of the Law, but by the faith of Jesus Christ, even we have believed in Jesus Christ that we might be justified by the faith of Christ and not by the works of the Law; for by the works of the Law shall no flesh be justified," Gal. 2, 16. Note the very definite, absolute barrier which Paul erects against works in giving us a description of justification. Hence prayer must not be thought of as forming part of justification. Probably somebody will here come with an objection and say: Your argumentation does not hold. Do you not see that St. Paul's description of justification requires something in man after all — faith? Works, then, are not excluded entirely; and prayer might enter in as well as faith. That reasoning may seem profound, but in reality is quite shallow. Faith has to do with justification not as a work, but merely as our receiving what God mercifully bestows on us. There is this peculiarity in faith, that it takes what God offers. It justifies not because it is a work of the Law, but because it grasps God's precious gift, the forgiveness of our sins. Prayer, however, is not a taking, it is an asking or a thanking. It is therefore radically different in its nature from faith and must not be confused with it or given the same function.

No, prayer belongs to sanctification, to the sanctified life with its many impulses, attitudes, thoughts, words, deeds, which follows inevitably after one has been justified. Put it before sanctification, and you are putting the cart before the horse; and while there may be tremendously much action, there will be no progress in the right direction. Consider that Jesus, when He in the Sermon on the Mount gives instruction on prayer, teaching His disciples the Lord's Prayer and encouraging them, "Ask, and it shall be given you," is speaking to people who have been justified and who are now to be told what sort of life they have to lead in their new state. Consider that it is the elect of God, holy and beloved, whom St. Paul admonishes (Col. 3, 12. 16 f.): "Let the Word of Christ dwell in you richly in all wisdom; teaching and admonishing one another in psalms and hymns and spiritual songs, singing with grace in your hearts to the Lord. And whatsoever ye do in word or deed, do all in the name of the Lord Jesus, giving thanks to God and the Father by Him."

So let us ever view our prayers. When we in our daily devotions and in the prayers offered in the church services appear before God, let this thought be definitely fixed in our minds, that, after God for Christ's sake has forgiven us our sins and justified us and we have taken this justification gratefully in true faith, we now stand before our heavenly Father in the relation of sinful but forgiven children, pouring out our hearts to Him, asking Him for what we need, and thanking Him for what He has graciously given us. Let us see, too, that our sincere prayers, while they may appear very insignificant, are something brought about in us, as was mentioned before, by the heavenly Visitor in our hearts, the Holy Spirit. Looked at in this light, as a part of sanctification produced by the Spirit of God, Christian prayer is grand and noble, a beautiful heavenly flower planted by the unseen divine Friend in our garden, showing that He is watching over us and blessing us.

XI

Prayer must not be regarded as something by means of which we merit, or deserve, salvation. At the risk of being charged with endeavoring to make a matter that has been fully demonstrated and is now quite clear still more clear, I am adding a special little chapter on the truth that by prayer we do not merit salvation. If there is anything that can destroy the beautiful, God-pleasing character of prayer, it is the idea that with our prayers we can deserve, or merit, the forgiveness of sins and eternal life. That belief would change it from a pious, Christian activity to a reprehensible, wicked undertaking. Forgiveness of sins and eternal life are gifts of God, which are bestowed on us freely. To say that we earn them is insulting the goodness and mercy of God. If a person became persistent in such a belief, it would terminate in the complete rejection on his part of the divine pardon and of the status of a child of God earned for him. Such a person would close to himself the doors to the heavenly home which Christ has opened to him.

One can hardly suppress the fear that many people pray with the very intention of wiping out their sin and conciliating the great and just God. As they have a wrong view of good works in general, so of prayer in particular. They lead a life of sin, and when finally their conscience smites them, a few sentences of prayer are to balance the scales of divine justice, so that no verdict of "guilty" will be pronounced. In fact, in the Roman Catholic Church, where good works are given a wrong status and are regarded as helping to procure for us the forgiveness of sins, prayer naturally is looked upon as a great factor in making us partakers of God's pardon. How utterly abominable this teaching is, which deprives the sinner of the assurance that Christ has earned for him everything that is required for our salvation, we can see from the anathema which the Apostle Paul hurls at the false teachers who beguiled the Galatian Christians into the belief that the keeping of the Law was at least in part necessary if they were to be justified. While I in this discussion wish to exalt prayer and picture it as glorious and necessary and effective, God forbid that I should say one word which would lead a person to believe that God's forgiveness is merited by it.

XII

While God has commanded us to pray, prayer must not be considered by us an irksome task, but a blessed privilege. God has commanded us to pray; that means, it is not left to our own desires whether we wish to engage in conversation with our God or not. He has told us that He expects us to commune with Him. "Pray without ceasing," His apostle tells us 1 Thess. 5, 17; and again: "I exhort therefore that first of all supplications, prayers, intercessions, and giving of thanks be made for all men," 1 Tim. 2, 1. And one of the beautiful parables of Jesus, usually called that of the importunate widow, is introduced with these words: "He spake a parable unto them to this end, that men ought always to pray and not to faint," Luke 18, 1. We observe, then, that, while God has left some matters in the sphere of religious life to our own choice, such as the keeping of days and the eating of, or abstaining from, certain foods, Rom. 14, 2 ff., prayer does not belong to this class.

And does not God's command that we pray agree perfectly with the relation which He sustains toward us and we toward Him, that He is our Father and that we are His children? Think of it. Through the sacrifice of His Son for us and through the work of the Holy Spirit in us God has made us His own. And now, after Bethlehem and Gethsemane and Golgotha and a Pentecost for every one of us, He should not desire that we, redeemed and sanctified, speak to Him about our wants and praise Him for what He has bestowed? Viewed in this light, prayer ought to be the most natural thing in the world for a Christian, and certainly there can be no surprise that God demands it of us. There is many a father who loves his children and does for their bodily and spiritual comfort whatever he is able to do. Does he wish that they communicate their wants and desires to him? And is he pleased if they receive his generous gifts one after the other without ever a word of acknowledgment, without a glad "Thank you"? We may have seen children who eat and drink at their father's table and enjoy the comforts of a well-furnished, beautiful home and the rest in a clean, inviting bed at night and the educational advantages which they should have, without any manifestation of gratitude and love on their part, who, on the contrary, are always pouting when they are at home and seem to have entered upon a thirty years' war against their parents. But where there are such sad cases, we recognize them as abnormal and shake our heads in bewilderment. Let us, then, see that in the relation which obtains between God and us He is not making unnatural demands when He orders us to pray, but is requesting exactly what we as children should expect Him to request.

How little, however, this last sentence does justice to the sentiments that should be expressed here! Yes, God has commanded us to pray, not, however, to put a laborious task on us, but to confer a great privilege. Prayer a task! What a caricature of it if we conceive of it as such! A father calls his children to his side and tells them, "Now ask for whatsoever you think you ought to have," and they consider this asking irksome toil! A king sends word to one of his subjects that he is to come for an audience and let his wants be known to his sovereign so they can be supplied, and he considers the going and the conversation to follow an unwelcome duty! It is to be feared that such is the view we often take of prayer, that, for instance, when in our Sunday services the pastor after the sermon begins to read the grand general prayer which so excellently mentions all our needs, many a person, far from being delighted and from devoutly joining in the petitions, inwardly grumbles at the many words he will now have to listen to and wonders how many seconds it will be before the Amen is reached. Such is the weakness of our flesh that we see burdens and labor and toil where we should see benefits, and favors, and advantages, and privileges.

XIII

The Scriptures give us the glorious assurance that God hears and answers prayer. In asserting that according to the Scriptures God hears and answers prayer, we come to one of the most important and most controverted aspects of our subject. Is Christian prayer effective or not? That is the question which here confronts us. We know that our praying is often ridiculed as a silly, useless, and absurd performance, which may possibly have some good influence on the one who prays, but can in no wise change the course of events or bring from the outside the aid which we require. Do you really think, we are asked, that prayer will cure tuberculosis and cancer, that it will prevent cyclones, tornadoes, dust-storms, and floods, that it will check invasions by locusts and chinch-bugs, that it will protect the soldier in battle against bullets and bayonet thrusts, that it will ward off accidents when you are traveling by train, auto, boat, or airship, that it will make you find and retain employment? So speaks the skeptic and unbeliever in taunting fashion, thinking that he is demonstrating the utter futility of our position.

In the *Christian Century*, several years ago, a contributor wrote these wicked words: "The views about God and the nature of the universe have changed. The element of petition in prayer, however carefully it may be phrased, is a work of the day when people actually did believe that God intervened directly to aid His friends and discomfit His enemies. Prayer was a specific means to a specific end. Our changing ideas of God make it impossible for us to believe in the efficacy of our prayers as we once did. For a few select souls there may be no difficulty, and they may be able to adjust themselves to relationships with this nebulous personality, personal goodness, essence of life, or however it may be designated; the majority of men, I believe, only fool themselves in thinking they can do it. Accordingly, as I see it, prayer in the conventional sense of the word is doomed as surely as burnt sacrifice and the Juggernaut car. Private meditation, a fresh taking stock of life, thanksgiving for the kindnesses we have received in not always reaping what we have sown, giving us, too, a more charitable attitude toward those who have had few buffers between themselves and failure and disgrace — these, yes. But the expectation of getting something for nothing or the readiness to request some one else to do what we know we ourselves ought to do — for this the knell has sounded."

Such are the venomous remarks of this writer. The pity of it is that he is not only attacking the Christian position, but is misrepresenting it. When he insinuates that our prayer is simply an ignoble attempt to get something for nothing or that it reflects the readiness to request some one else to do what we know we ourselves ought to do, he is presenting a caricature of prayer which every Christian realizes is as little like the reality as a Russian thistle is like an elm-tree.

We cannot prevent these enemies from mouthing their spite

against what we hold sacred, but we can, with the help of the Holy Spirit, fortify our hearts against surrender to such destructive views. Our chief means of defense is the Word of God with its beautiful promises, guaranteeing to us that God hears and answers our prayers. Our hearts ought to leap for joy as we think of these sweet, comforting, uplifting passages of the Scriptures.

"Call upon Me in the day of trouble; I will deliver thee, and thou shalt glorify Me," Ps. 50, 15, is the grand assurance given us by God through the psalmist. "Ask, and it shall be given you; seek, and ye shall find; knock, and it shall be opened unto you. For every one that asketh, receiveth; and he that seeketh, findeth; and to him that knocketh it shall be opened," Matt. 7, 7 f., is the clear, definite promise given us by our divine Savior Himself. And again He says: "All things whatsoever ye shall ask in prayer, believing, ye shall receive," Mark 11, 24. These are passages which are quoted in our Catechism, and we are quite familiar with them; but surely our having known them from the days of childhood does not deprive them of their beautiful, comforting significance. They deserve that we make them the daily diet of our soul, keeping it thereby from becoming famished, weak and faint, and unable to endure the temptations and afflictions in this vale of tears. Whatever views a person may have concerning the Bible, whether one exalts it as the infallible Scriptures, as we do, or whether people in blind ignorance look upon it as being merely another book, a sheaf of documents that have no more value than other records of the remote past, one cannot deny that there is here placed before us in unequivocal language the promise that God will hear and answer our prayers. In days of doubt, of disappointment, of sorrow, when the dark clouds of misfortune and disaster have massed themselves directly above us and the sun of joy and hope apparently has faded from the universe and not the faintest ray of hope is discernible, then let us cling to these promises of our great God and say, after all: He who does not lie or deceive has declared that He will hear us in the day of trouble and listen as we with trembling hands knock at His door. So we shall pray and firmly believe that our praying will not be in vain.

That there are many other passages of the same import is known to every Bible-reader, and as we proceed, there will be an opportunity to draw attention to one or the other of them.

XIV

That these promises of God, assuring us that He hears the prayers of His children, are true is shown by many instances reported in the Bible and in the history of the Church. When we talk to each other of actual occurrences which testify that God's promises with respect to our prayers are not worthless, we open another comforting and uplifting chapter. Thinking first of the Scriptures, we cannot review all the narratives reporting that God heard petitions of His saints. It will have to suffice that attention is drawn to a few conspicuous examples. Let us think of the case of Abraham. In a most remarkable passage we are told how he earnestly pleaded with God for the preservation of Sodom, the wicked city in which Lot dwelt, and that the Lord did not look upon this prayer as presumption, but when Abraham became more and more bold in his intercession and reduced the number of just people on whose account he asked the Lord not to destroy the city finally to ten, he received the assurance, "I shall not destroy it for ten's sake," Gen. 18, 32. It is true, Sodom was destroyed, the reason being not that Abraham's prayer was not effective, but that there were not even ten righteous persons in the city. Think of Moses. When Pharaoh pursued the children of Israel with his chariots, his horsemen, and the rest of his army and it appeared that Israel was doomed, Moses called upon God for help, and, behold, the sea divided and Israel, without pontoons, rafts, canoes, or ships, effected a passage to the other side, while their enemies following them were led into a watery grave. Think of Samuel. The Philistines had gathered their hosts against the poor Israelites, who were no match for them; but the prophet prayed to God for his people, and the account says: "The Lord thundered with a great thunder on that day upon the Philistines and discomfited them, and they were smitten before Israel," 1 Sam. 7, 10. Then there are the cases of David, Jehoshaphat, Elijah, Elisha, and Hezekiah, to mention but a few of the men of God whose prayers were crowned with visible, tangible results. In the New Testament lepers approach Jesus with a prayer for cleansing, and they are healed. The centurion asks for his servant who was at the point of death, and from a distance, without seeing him, Jesus grants him recovery. The Syrophenician woman asks for her daughter who was grievously vexed by the devil, and when she returns home from her interview with Christ, she finds that her prayer has been answered. Peter is in prison, awaiting the death-sentence and execution; his friends pray for him, and the angel of God leads him forth from between soldiers guarding him. Paul and Silas are in prison and pray, and an earthquake opens the prison-doors, and their bands are loosed. What a grand list of instances recorded in the Scriptures where prayer was answered in a striking, noticeable way we could draw up!

When we go into church history, we find many examples of this kind handed down. Famous is the case of Luther's praying for Melanchthon, which is reported in these words by Patton (*Prayer and Its Remarkable Answers*, p. 243): "The prayer of Luther for the recovery of Melanchthon, who was apparently at the point of death, is well known to every student of the history of the Reformation. Melanchthon's learning and facile pen were invaluable to the cause, while his milder manner avoided the offense often given by Luther's impetuosity and occasional coarseness [?]. Hence, when Luther was summoned to the death-bed of his dearly loved friend, he burst into tears and an exclamation of agony. This aroused Melanchthon, who said, 'O Luther, is this you? Why don't you let me depart in peace?' 'We can't spare you yet, Philip,' was the Reformer's answer. And then he spent more than an hour on his knees, pleading for his recovery, until he felt that his prayer was heard. Then he turned to Melanchthon again, whom he took by the hand, and who said, 'Dear Luther, why don't you let me depart in peace?' and received as an answer, 'No, no, Philip, we cannot spare you yet from the field of labor.' Luther had some soup brought and, when his friend declined it, saying, 'Dear Luther, why will you not let me go home?' again replied, 'We cannot spare you yet, Philip,' and added in his droll way, 'Philip, take this soup, or I will excommunicate you.' The soup was taken, Melanchthon began to revive, and he lived to labor many years. When Luther went home, he told his wife with triumphant joy, 'God gave me my brother Melanchthon back in direct answer to prayer.'" Patton adds: "Can any one doubt this who considers the promises of God and the peculiar circumstances of the case?"

There is another story related about Luther which shows the power of Christian prayer. One of his contemporaries and valiant coworkers was a pastor by the name of Myconius, who labored in Gotha and Leipzig. When this man was very ill, he said that he was ready to depart, but that he would like to see his paternal friend Luther once more. Growing weaker, he finally, with trembling hand, wrote a letter of farewell to Luther. When the great Reformer received this communication, he exclaimed, "God cannot permit this." At once he wrote a letter to Myconius which is truly startling in its bold confidence: "No, you diligent worker in the business of the Lord dare not be called away as yet. I command you in the name of God to live because I need you still for the reformation of the Church. May the Lord not let me hear while I live that you have died, but may He bring it about that you survive me! That is what I pray for earnestly, and it is my will that it be granted and come to pass and that my will be done. Amen. For this my will seeks the glory of the divine name, not my own glory or pleasure; that is certainly true. Once more I say, May God keep you! From the bottom of our heart we pray for you, and your illness causes us not little anxiety and grief. Written on the Sunday after Epiphany, in the year 1541." Heroic words they were. When the letter arrived and was read to Myconius, he was no longer able to speak. But at once he began to recover. Not many weeks afterwards he was able to visit Luther in Wittenberg. When people expressed their joy at seeing that he had been spared, he replied: "Yes, my friends, next to our all-merciful Father in heaven I owe this extension of my life to Martin Luther, this hero in prayer, who can by faith obtain everything from God. His mighty word has restored me, who am of feeble constitution, similarly as the command of Jesus raised Lazarus." While Myconius never again was of robust health, he actually survived Luther by several months.

A few more instances of this kind ought to be mentioned here. A man whose memory deserves being kept live and fresh is August Herman Francke. Holding the position of pastor and professor at Halle, he devoted much time to the bodily and, especially, spiritual care of neglected children and sheltered as many of them in his own house as possible. To carry on this work on a large scale, he built an orphanage. It was the beginning of a number of charitable and educational institutions which are known as the Francke Foundations and have aroused the admiration of the world. Having no means himself, he had to support the undertaking through gifts of charity. His own account shows how much and what marvelous things were accomplished by prayer.

"In the month of April, 1696, our funds were exhausted, and

I knew not where to look for the necessary supplies for the next week. This caused me great distress, when some person, who is yet unknown to me, put into my hands a thousand dollars for the orphans. At another time, when our stores were exhausted, we laid our case before the Lord and had scarcely finished our prayer, when there was a knock at my door, and a letter was handed in with fifty dollars in gold. Twenty dollars soon after came, which fully supplied our wants, and we were taught that God will often hear prayer almost before it is offered. In the month of October, 1698, I sent a ducat to a poor and afflicted woman, who wrote me that it came to hand at a time when she greatly needed it, and she prayed God to give my poor orphans a heap of ducats for it. Soon after, I received from one friend two ducats; from another, twenty-five; from two others, forty-three; and from Prince Paul of Wurttemberg, five hundred. When I saw all this money on the table before me, I could not but think of the prayer of the poor woman and how literally it had been fulfilled.

"In February, 1699, I was almost entirely without funds, though much was needed for the daily wants of the children and other poor. In this state of difficulty I comforted myself with the promise of the Lord Jesus 'Seek ye first the kingdom,' etc. When I had given out the last of our money, I prayed to the Lord. As I left my room to go into the college, I found a student waiting for me, who put seventy dollars into my hand. Soon afterwards we were in the greatest want, but I trusted in the Lord and determined to go to my closet and spread my wants before Him. I arose to go to my closet, and while I was on my way, a letter was put into my hands from a merchant, who informed me that he had received a check for a thousand dollars to be paid me for the orphan home. How forcibly did I feel the truth of the promise 'Before they call, I will answer, and while they are yet speaking, I will hear.' I had now no reason to ask for assistance, but I went to my closet and praised the Lord for His goodness. At another time the superintendent of the building came to me and asked if I had received any money for paying the laborers. 'No,' said I; 'but I have faith in God.' Scarcely had I uttered these words when some one was announced at the door. On going to him, I found that he had brought me thirty dollars. I returned to the study and asked the superintendent how much money he needed. He replied, 'Thirty dollars.' 'There they are,' said I. At another time of great need I prayed particularly, 'Give us this day our daily bread.' I dwelt upon the words 'this day,' for we needed aid immediately. While I was yet praying, a friend came to my door and brought me four hundred dollars.

"At one time I was recounting to a Christian friend some of our remarkable deliverances from want, by which he was so much affected that he even wept. While I was speaking, as if to confirm my statements, I received a letter containing a check for five hundred dollars. At another time I was in need of a large sum, but did not know where to obtain even ten dollars. The steward came, but, having no money for him, I asked him to come again after dinner and in the mean time gave myself to prayer. When he came, in the afternoon, all I could do was to ask him to come again in the evening. In the afternoon I was visited by a friend, with whom I united in prayer to God. As I accompanied my friend to the door on his departure, I found the steward standing on one side and on the other a person who put into my hands a hundred and fifty dollars. On another occasion the superintendent began to pay the laborers with only fourteen dollars, but before he got through, he received enough to complete the pay ments." (Cf. Patton, *op. cit.*, 385—388.)

In Bristol, England, George Mueller built orphan homes, encouraged by the example of Francke. He, too, was a poor man, and he says that by prayer and faith, without asking any individuals, he obtained the required means for this undertaking. Some of his words should be quoted. In one of his reports he says: "What cannot God do in answer to believing, expecting prayer! Dear Christian reader, seek to rely upon God increasingly, and you will see how blessed it is to do so under all circumstances. I have walked by God's grace in this happy road for forty-five years and six months, out of the forty-nine years and eight months during which I have been a believer, and on these principles, 'Trust in the living God and prayer,' this institution has been carried on for forty-one years, during which time, without applying to any one, I have received, simply in answer to believing prayer, the sum of £665,000 [in our money $3,325,000]."

In 1935, when the seventieth anniversary of the death of Louis Harms was dwelt on in the papers, attention was drawn also to a number of remarkable instances in his life when his prayers were heard. One of his dear friends was smitten by severe illness.

The doctor declared the case hopeless. The wife of the patient, a woman of strong faith, announced that she would go to see Pastor Harms, who lived at a considerable distance. It appeared as though she had been impelled by a strange vagary to leave her husband while he was on his death-bed. When she reached Harms, she and this man of God engaged in prayer. The sick man immediately began to recover, and when on the day after the visit of this Christian woman at Harms's house the physician called on his patient, thinking he might probably ease his sufferings a little, the man, to his great surprise, met him at the door fully restored to health. The physician is said to have stated it as his conviction that a miracle had occurred. The former patient said: "This is not all. On my leg I had a cancerous growth, which a number of physicians to whom I applied for aid were not able to heal. It is now completely gone. He showed the place to the physician, who was much amazed. The day after, the woman returned home in good spirits. She knew that her prayer had been answered, and she had not worried. (Cf. *Der christliche Apologete,* Sept. 18, 1935.)

Harms's prayer manifested its efficacy especially in connection with his great mission venture among the heathen. Filled with burning desire to bring the Gospel to those sitting in darkness and the shadow of death, he established a mission house for the education of missionaries. When the missionaries had been trained and there was no mission society which was ready to take them into its service, he built a mission ship, *Candace,* to take his emissaries to Africa, a ship which carried missionaries and supplies for more than twenty years. Besides, he founded a mission journal to create interest in this cause, and of course he supported the missionaries, both those who were sent originally and such as were added later. How God heard his prayers he himself relates in these words (Patton, *op. cit.,* p. 389): "A short time ago I had to pay a merchant in behalf of the missions 550 crowns, and when the day was near, I had only 400. Then I prayed to the Lord Jesus that He would provide me with the deficiency. On the day before, three letters were brought, one from Schweim with 20, one from Buecksburg with 25, and one from Berlin with 100 crowns. The donors were anonymous. On the evening of the same day a laborer brought me 10 crowns; so that I had not only enough, but 5 over. — I must tell you what brought tears into my eyes and confirmed me anew in that word 'Before they call, I will answer.' A medicine-chest was urgently wanted for the mission. I reckoned up to see if there was enough left to supply it. Before I had finished, and when I had not yet well begun to commend this matter to the Lord, a letter was brought in which the anonymous writer stated that for some time he had been collecting for the mission and had determined to purchase a medicine-chest. The chest accompanied the letter; he only begged it might soon be sent out to the heathen."

In this fashion I could continue to relate instances from the lives of children of God showing that the Father in heaven hears and anwsers our prayers.

XV

The objection that such a view of the efficacy of prayer is contrary to God's eternal decrees is not tenable. We now have to begin a series of chapters of saddening import, because we have to look at the objections which have been, and are being, raised against the clear teaching of God's Word on the significance of prayer, and we have to deal with the attempts made by human ingenuity to overthrow the comforting assurances of the Scriptures. An objection which is heard quite often is reported by Dr. Walther (*Gnadenjahr,* p. 169 f.) in these words: "People say from eternity it has been decreed what is to happen, and who now can imagine that by his prayer he is able to bring about a change in the divine plan according to which the world is governed? Who dare hope through prayer to make the unchangeable God hesitant and to induce Him to alter His will?" When a person hears this objection, it sounds formidable. But Dr. Walther effectually disposes of it. "These people do not consider that God can hear all our prayers without acting contrary to His eternal decrees; for since God is omniscient and all-wise, He not only from eternity knew that we would pray and what would be the objectives of our prayer, but from eternity He has so arranged everything and given it its place in His government of the universe that those very things must come to pass which we request of Him." This must silence the critics who oppose us with a reference to the eternal decrees of God. The very quality in God which, they think, militates against our belief with respect to the efficacy of prayer we appeal to in showing that their objection is futile. The critics merely betray that they are not consistent enough in speaking of God's omniscient guidance and drawing arguments from it.

XVI

The objection that God's granting of our petitions is made impossible by the existence of laws of nature which operate with absolute regularity is likewise ill founded. It is strange that people will gather up all their strength and lie awake at night to devise arguments by means of which they can prove what they consider the futility of prayer, whereas they should rather joyfully use their powers of intellect to demonstrate that prayer is a mighty instrument given us by God for our good. It reminds one of the Jews, who, when our Lord Jesus Christ walked visibly in their midst, held councils, not to consider how they might keep Him with them as long as possible in His role of Teacher and Healer and general Benefactor, but how they might get rid of Him as quickly and effectually as expediency would allow. In their attempts to discredit prayer, the enemies of the Scriptures have turned their attention to the laws of nature and have fancied that from them they might obtain some ammunition with which to attack the Bible-teaching on the efficacy of prayer. The laws of nature, embodying what we know of cause and effect in the world about us, such as the law of gravitation, of motion, of light, and of sound, are held to operate with unfailing precision and to permit of no suspension of their activity as a result of our prayers. A man is falling down from the roof of a high building; there he is in the air; the force of gravity is pulling him downward, and no amount of praying will keep him up high above the earth, we are told. There are loose particles of dust lying on the ground in the so-called dust-bowl of the United States; a wind begins to blow, and no deluge of prayers can protect these dust particles from being swept away from their native home into regions where they will be frowned on as unwelcome visitors. There is a huge fire, and however numerous or fervent the prayers you utter, they will be unable to deprive the flames of heat and destructive force. A man runs into the path of a twentieth-century passenger train rushing along at the rate of one hundred miles an hour, and pray as you will, the tremendous momentum of that train with its power to crush men and cattle usurping its right of way will not be diminished. So runs the objection.

On superficial consideration it might seem indeed as though here there had been advanced a criticism of our doctrine of the efficacy of prayer which we would have to permit to stand. We are undeniably living in a universe of law and order. What you sow you will reap. And if you do not sow, you won't reap. The sun rises on the evil and the good, and rain falls on the lands of the just and the unjust. Indeed, as God Himself has said, seedtime and harvest, cold and heat, summer and winter, day and night, are following each other in ever-revolving cycles. In a world where the course of events is so dependent on natural causes, where eclipses can be predicted with absolute accuracy, and where weather forecasts tell us in advance of the coming storms, is not prayer just as puny and insignificant as a feather with which you endeavor to oppose the progress of a tornado? Hence we are told, When you are hungry and your body is growing weak, the remedy is not prayer, but partaking of a meal. When there is a contagious disease raging in your vicinity, you avoid being stricken not by praying fervently, but by observing the respective rules of sanitation. The captain taking his vessel from San Francisco to Sydney avoids shipwreck not by the power of prayer, but by steering a course which has been found unobstructed by hidden reefs and treacherous shoals. Human observation seems to bear out that, as this world is constituted, there is no room in it for prayer.

But substantial as this objection may seem to be, it cannot overthrow our conviction that God hears and answers prayer. In fact, I have no doubt that every mature, intelligent Christian, though he perhaps has not reflected on this matter in the very terms which I have used, has come to grips with the difficulty which has been pointed to and has triumphantly conquered it. He has said to himself that, though this is a universe of orderly arrangement, a kosmos where everything has its proper place and function, our God is not bound by the laws and forces which He has created, but that He can use them according to His will; that He is not their slave and subject, but their Master. He has come to see that, while there are natural forces which bring about certain results, God can easily bring in other forces to neutralize the effect of the former; that, for instance, while the winds will drive the dust before them which happens to be lying in their path, God can send rains to keep those little particles of earth on the ground where we like to see them remain. The Christian realizes the truth of what has well been said in reply to the argument we are discussing: "The commonplace objection to prayer founded on the supposed immutability of the laws by which God governs the world is easily met and answered by the fact that prayer is itself one of these laws upon whose working God has determined that a certain result shall follow." (Quoted by Zwemer, *Taking Hold of God*, p. 70.) Yes, just as little as one can eliminate God from the universe by saying that this is a world of well-arranged and balanced forces, so little can one shut out from it the power and influence of prayer. You say that abundant snowfall in the Sierra Nevada has beneficent results for the slopes, plains, and valleys of California, which thereby in the dry season are furnished the moisture which they need. So consider prayer as a gentle snowfall on the hills surrounding the City of God whence there flow help and supplies in times of need.

A few illustrations from the New Testament may here be serviceable. Jesus and His disciples are crossing the Sea of Galilee, and a sudden storm of extraordinary violence breaks upon them. The disciples appeal to Jesus for help. Their prayer is efficacious; Jesus comes to their aid, He performs an astounding miracle. But how? Not by seizing them and carrying them through the air to the shore, as He could have done, but by making the storm cease and the waters be still. Using our present-day scientific terminology, we might say He made the atmospheric pressure abate and thus caused the rapid air currents to stop, and everything grew quiet. We see clearly that He is the Master of nature and can marshal its forces to do His will. When Paul as a prisoner was making the famous voyage to Rome related in Acts 27 and 28 and a hurricane tossed the ship about on the Mediterranean like a little shell and disaster appeared inevitable, we can be sure that Paul and Luke engaged in earnest prayer for their preservation and that of their companions. God gave Paul the assurance that the lives of all on board would be saved, and this was brought about. But how? Not by the appearance of a legion of angels who took the passengers and the crew into their arms and carried them to Italy, — a method that God could have employed, — but by God's governing the forces of nature in such a way that the ship came close enough to an island to permit all it carried, when it ran aground and was broken to pieces by the billows, to reach the shore in safety. The story confirms our belief that God is not powerless over against the gigantic elemental forces that we observe in the world, but that He governs them in keeping with the prayers of His children, and they have to be the means of accomplishing His will. Whoever believes that there is an almighty and omnipresent God will have no difficulty in accepting this teaching.

XVII

The objection that many Christian prayers are not heard rests on a misapprehension and does not disprove the efficacy of our prayer. The enemies of the joyous belief that prayer accomplishes great things take recourse to the realm of experience. The universe is filled with the wrecks of unheard prayers, we are told. Quite likely the critic will first take material from the Bible itself, saying: "Think of James the Elder, whom Herod Agrippa beheaded, Acts 12. Shall we assume that the congregation did not pray for him? We are told it offered up prayers for the safety of Peter, which were granted. Do you think it likely that they neglected to pray for the preservation of James? Behold, he was taken to the place of execution and put to death. Or take the case of Jesus Himself. He prayed: 'Father, if it be possible, let this cup pass from Me; nevertheless, not as I will, but as Thou wilt.' His prayer that He might be spared the bitter cup certainly was sincere; but He had to empty the cup to the very dregs. Paul is being tempted by a thorn in the flesh. The messenger of Satan buffets him; three times he implores the Lord that the affliction might leave him, but, as he himself admits, his prayer was not granted, 2 Cor. 12, 7—9." Then the critic will probably continue: "Think of what happens every day. There are millions of Christians who stand at the bedside of a dear member of their family that is ill; they pray fervently for the recovery of that beloved person, but the angel of death comes nevertheless. There are thousands upon thousands of devout Christians lying on a bed of pain and crying to God for relief, but their pain and misery continue. There were millions of farmers, many of them true children of God, who in drought-stricken areas prayed for rain, and the moisture they asked for and their land needed was not supplied." So speaks the critic, and the question we have to answer is whether, after all, it is not a mistake to regard the true efficacy of prayer to consist in this, that we thereby obtain things we ask for, and whether we ought not rather to say that by prayer a change is brought about in us, a change which makes us submit to the will of God and gladly bear what is put on us. This is the much-quoted view of F. W. Robertson, the famous English minister who lived one hundred years ago in Brighton, England, and whose sermons are still widely read.

We reply: Here as elsewhere the critics of the divine Word

are in error and are misled by their ingenuity. From their observation that some prayers are not fulfilled in the manner which the petitioner has mentioned they conclude that these prayers have not been heard and answered at all. That is a thoroughly unjustified inference. A boy on a trip asks his father for a box of chocolates because he is hungry and, besides, is particularly fond of chocolates. The father fetches him an ordinary ham or cheese sandwich. He has heard and granted the prayer of his little son, not of course in the precise manner which the latter suggested, but in the manner which was best for the boy. That the preservation of the life of James, the son of Zebedee, was prayed for by his fellow-Christians we assume. These prayers were heard and fulfilled in such a way that the best interests of James and his cobelievers were served. His work here on earth, we can be sure, was finished, and God took him into the heavenly home to enjoy the Sabbath of the children of God. You might say that God gave these Christians more than they had asked for. What they desired for James was the lengthening of his earthly life. God granted him the entrance upon everlasting life instead. — Paul's prayer for the removal of the thorn in the flesh, consisting probably of malaria or an eye disease or some other physical malady, certainly was heard because he himself records what God said to him in reply to his request. You have what is good for you, the Lord said in effect; you have My grace; consider that sufficient. Be content to be weak because it is just through weak vessels that I perform My work. And Paul firmly believed that his prayer had been heard and answered. He was happy and declared himself willing to glory in the very weakness which before he had asked to be relieved of. When we approach the divine mystery of Jesus' prayer in the Garden of Gethsemane, we ought first to take off our shoes because we are standing on holy ground. The real depths of this matter we shall never fathom while we are here on earth. That Jesus' prayer was heard is the express statement of the Scriptures in Heb. 5, 7 f.: "Jesus in the days of His flesh, when He had offered up prayers and supplications with strong crying and tears unto Him that was able to save Him from death and was heard in that He feared, though He were a Son, yet learned He obedience by the things which He suffered." You note the definite statement: He was heard. We put this down as an absolute fact. We note furthermore that Jesus by no means *demanded* removal of the bitter cup. The answer to the question whether He could and should be spared the suffering that was rushing down upon Him He placed entirely into the hands of His heavenly Father. The prayer which He uttered was heard. An angel came and strengthened Him. Without faltering, without the shadow of disobedience, Jesus let Himself be led into the dark valley of unspeakable anguish and death; and on the third day He rose triumphantly from the grave and the great work of redemption was attested as accomplished. Yes, Jesus was heard, His prayer was granted, not, it is true, in the way in which we probably should have expected it to be granted, but in a way which was in agreement with the great counsels of God and the requirements of our eternal salvation.

Concerning these cases that we have just considered, I ought to say one word more. There is taught in them, besides other valuable lessons, this important truth, that our prayers at times, perhaps even often, are fulfilled in such a manner that we do not notice the fulfilment at once, if at all. That God heard the prayer of St. Paul when he in deep distress cried for a cessation of the onslaughts of Satan's messenger and these buffetings continued, who that witnessed this struggle could perceive? Imagine that Timothy heard the apostle wrestling in prayer with God. On general principles he would have said that this praying was not in vain, but he would have been compelled to add, till informed by St. Paul after the divine answer had been received, that he was not able to see that the fervent pleading was crowned with success. A Christian business man, having climbed to great heights in the financial and industrial world, through no fault of his own is confronted with the peril of bankruptcy. He prays devoutly to be spared such a calamity; but the collapse comes, and he loses everything he has in his attempt to satisfy his creditors. To the end of his life he remains a poor man and never again cuts any sort of figure in the financial world. People who knew with what earnestness he approached the throne of God in the hours of impending humiliation will be inclined to say that God did not hear and grant his prayer. He himself probably to the end of his life, while having unalterable trust that God's ways are right and for our good, will be unable to demonstrate that God heard and helped him at that time. In yonder world the mystery may be unlocked for him, and he may learn that he through his business success had been carried perilously near to the edge of puffed-up conceitedness and self-sufficient pride and that his case required heroic measures, a major operation, which the divine Physician in mercy performed. What is important for us to see is that our failure to discern, distinctly or faintly, the fulfilment of our petitions must not be regarded as proof that they have not been heard and favorably acted upon.

A famous instance in point is that of Monica, the mother of St. Augustine, who prayed for the conversion of her son. Since she believed that her influence upon him was an essential factor, she earnestly besought God not to let Augustine depart from Africa, a thing he was contemplating doing. In Book V of his *Confessions,* Augustine describes the event I have alluded to: "Why I left here [that is, Africa] and went there [that is, Italy] Thou knewest, O God. Thou didst indicate it, however, neither to me nor to my mother, who mourned about me vehemently and followed me to the sea. But I deceived her when she was tenaciously clinging to me that she might either bring me back or go with me; and I pretended to be unwilling to leave a friend till he with the coming of a favorable wind would set sail. And I told a lie to my mother, and such a mother at that, and I escaped, because Thou also mercifully forgavest me, preserving me from the water of the sea, full of execrable uncleanness as I was, [and keeping me] for the water of Thy grace, by which, when I had been washed, the floods of my mother's eyes were to be dried up, with which floods she daily before Thee moistened the earth beneath her. When she refused to return home without me, I with difficulty persuaded her to stay that night in a place which was very close to our ship, the mausoleum of the blessed Cyprian. But in that very night I secretly started out while she remained there praying and weeping. And what, my God, was she asking of Thee with so many tears if not that Thou shouldest not let me sail? But Thou, according to Thy high counsel and hearing well the chief import of that supplication, didst not provide what she was asking for at that time in order to make me that which she was always asking for. The wind blew and filled our sails and took away the shore from our view, where in the morning she was beside herself with pain and with lamentations and groanings filled Thy ears that were heedless of such things, while Thou (in reality) wert carrying me off through my lusts in order to put an end to these very lusts and to let her carnal desire be chastened by the just scourge of pains. For she longed for my presence with her after the fashion of mothers, but much more than many others, and she was not aware what joy Thou wert intending to cause her through my absence. She was not aware of it; therefore she wept and lamented, and in this grief there manifested itself in her the inheritance of Eve, since with pain she sought what with pain she had given birth to. And after accusing my falseness and cruelty, she nevertheless turned again to plead with Thee for me and went back to her usual tasks while I went to Rome." Yes, apparently God did not hear the earnest, fervent prayer of Monica; but in reality He did hear it. For by permitting Augustine to go to Italy, He brought him in contact with Ambrose in Milan, through whose ministry the wayward son was converted.

Let us look at the matter from another side. Knowing that our God is omnipotent, we do not doubt for a moment that He could grant what we, His children, ask for, though it appear ever so impossible. When Moses asked God to let him see His glory, the Lord could have vouchsafed him such a vision. But often God does not give us what we request, not because He cannot, but because He must not give it, since our welfare and that of others forbids His granting us our petitions. Moses was very short-sighted and more zealous than prudent when he asked to be shown God's glory. God told him: "Thou canst not see My face, for there shall no man see Me and live," Ex. 33, 20. If God had approached Moses with His majesty in full visibility, the prophet would have perished at once. When the poor demoniac whom Jesus had freed from a legion of demons asked that he might be permitted to accompany Jesus, the Lord could of course have granted him that favor. But it would not have been for the best of his fellow-men. There were people sitting in darkness in that man's village and the surrounding territory who needed to be told the Gospel-message. So instead of yielding, Jesus sent him back to his people as a bearer of good tidings.

Are instances of this kind altogether rare nowadays? A man may ask God to give him employment. He has his mind fixed on a certain position which, he thinks, would be very suitable for him and yield the income he needs. He does not get the position. It appears as though God did not hear his request. Future developments, however, may show that it would have been ruinous for this man both from the financial and from the spiritual point of view if he had received the position he desired, there being perils connected with it of which he did not dream. We must recognize that our prayers are not always wise. We map out a plan for ourselves; later years may show that we should have been led into disaster if the plan had been put into effect. In such cases God does not grant our request, not because He cannot, but because He must not do it from the point of view of our real welfare.

It has been thought that a sure proof of the futility of prayer is found in the fact that at times Christian people are praying for directly opposite things, some for rain, others, living in the same locality, for dry weather; some for high, others for low prices; some, if we transport ourselves back to 1914, for victory of the French, others for victory of the German arms. If God hears the one side, He must refuse the petition of the other, it has been said. Granting the prayer of Mr. Smith, who lives on the upland, for abundant moisture, he cannot bestow on his neighbor Mr. Jones, in the bottoms, what the latter asks for, a long dry season. If He permits the Germans victoriously to march into Paris, he cannot grant the urgent prayer of French Christians that their capital may not fall into the hands of the enemy. Yes, we say, this objection would hold if the efficacy of our prayers meant that God always gives us precisely what we ask for. Let a person see clearly that our prayers by no means are meant to dethrone God and to take the government of the universe out of His hands, but that our petitions are an appeal to Him for help and that they by no means prescribe to Him in which way He is to furnish the help we need, and the objection will fall to the ground. The poet Longfellow is quoted to have said: "What discord should we bring into the universe if our prayers were all answered! Then we should govern the world, and not God. And do you think we should govern it better? It gives me only pain when I hear the long, wearisome petitions of men asking for they know not what." The rebuke implied in these words of Longfellow is justified if we, in telling God of our needs, imagine we can inform Him on the best method of furnishing us with what our welfare requires. But that such an intention is far removed from the mind of every true, humble child of God we know very well. We say, then, God hears and answers the prayers of His children living in opposite camps and praying for opposite gifts, not of course always in the manner in which they would like to have them answered, but in such way as serves the best interests of all. A saying of Luther from his *Table Talk* is *apropos:*

"We have this advantage, that God always hears our prayer. For if it is not granted according to our will, it is granted according to the will of God, which is better than our own. And if I did not know that my prayer is heard, then the devil might pray in my stead. It is not necessary that God should always grant my petitions according to my will; for in that case He would be in my control and my prisoner; and why should He grant what we ask for if He has better insight into our needs than we?" We must bear in mind, too, that probably our prayer appears unanswered to us because we wish to see results immediately while our God, for our own good, delays, sending us the relief requested later. How wrong to say that such a prayer was not heard!

Another thought may well be expressed here. At times people gain the impression that Christian prayers are not answered because they forget or overlook that there are higher and better gifts than robust health, a lucrative position, a splendid farm, a fat purse, a well-paying government job, and the like; that far superior to all of them are the gifts of the Spirit, the Holy Spirit Himself and the inward blessings He bestows: faith, hope, love, righteousness, peace, joy, comfort and strength in tribulation, and a serene, happy death. There is a person who as a permanent invalid is confined to a bed of pain. All his prayers for restoration of his health apparently have been in vain. If, however, we had eyes that we could see what is taking place in the spiritual world, we should notice that on that sick-bed constantly gifts of God are descending; that the patient is made strong in faith, ardent in hope, rich in knowledge of the Scriptures, wise in the counsels of God, tender in his affections, diligent in prayer; that in his infirmity he becomes a mighty witness for Christ and His love to all who approach his sick-bed; that instead of being a burden, he is a valuable asset to his family and the congregation to which he belongs. Certainly his prayers have been heard and have been answered, not through God's bestowing what the world calls the greatest boon, but what from the point of view of the kingdom of God and eternity must be most highly prized.

And these spiritual blessings, so we always should remind ourselves, we may ask for with a full assurance that here our judgment is not mistaken in making its request. In Luke 11, 13 the Savior says: "If ye, then, being evil, know how to give good gifts unto your children, how much more shall your heavenly Father give the Holy Spirit to them that ask Him!" When we approach

our heavenly Father for temporal blessings, good health, profitable
employment, a favorable season, we have to be mindful of our
short-sightedness, realizing that what we ask for may, after all,
not be what we ought to receive in the given situation; that, if
we knew all circumstances and could look far ahead, we probably
should utter an altogether different petition; that hence we should
leave the granting of our prayer entirely to the wisdom and love
of God, who will not give us a stone instead of bread, a serpent
instead of a fish, a scorpion instead of an egg. "Lord, if Thou
wilt, if Thou seest that it is good for me and will not work harm
to my fellow-men," that should be included whenever our prayer
is a petition for things of this earthly life. Let the distinction
which I have just drawn be kept in view, and there will be less
talk about unfulfilled petitions. We may, then, in viewing all
that has been said on unanswered prayer, put the matter thus by
way of summary: God hears all the prayers of His children and
takes the action required. This action, it is true, may remain
unnoticed by us, or it may be different from what we expect and
desire; but it will always be for our good; it will serve what is
highest in our existence, our spiritual well-being, the right relation
to God, our being believers in Jesus Christ. Somebody has
expressed it in these beautiful words, speaking of a praying
Christian:

"He asked for strength that he might achieve — he was made
weak that he might obey.

"He asked for health that he might do *greater* things — he
was given infirmity that he might do *better* things.

"He asked for riches that he might be happy — he was given
poverty that he might be wise.

"He asked for power that he might have praise of men —
he was given weakness that he might feel the need of God.

"He asked for all things that he might enjoy life — he was
given 'life' that he might enjoy all things.

"He received nothing that he asked for or hoped for — his
prayer was answered." (Quoted by W. L. Hannam in *Luke the
Evangelist*, p. 153. The Abingdon Press.)

How true! Often God's answer to our prayer is a refusal to
grant our request; instead of saying yes, He says no; and it is
the very best answer under the circumstances, the very answer we
need. His name be praised!

XVIII

Prayer must not be considered a sort of magic by means of which we obtain what we desire or a substitute for the faithful use of our bodily and mental faculties in meeting our problems. Enemies of Christian prayer at times charge that we regard prayer as a magical device by means of which we can provide for ourselves what we need. In magic, as the term usually is defined, the only thing that you have to do is to use a certain formula, speak the word, make the sign, and, so it is alleged, at once the wished-for result springs into being. Those people who say that for us prayer is something magical have learned that, if you wish to discredit a thing, it is helpful if you call it bad names and give it some disreputable label. So they turn to abuse. Every mature, intelligent Christian knows that his view of prayer is not such as here described. It may be, however, that there are some people who actually use prayer as if it belonged to the magical arts. They do not think of pouring out their hearts to God and appearing before Him with thanksgiving and telling Him of their needs as a child does in speaking to its father. But when trouble comes knocking strongly at their door and they see no way out, they have recourse to prayer. For them prayer is merely a supernatural device for obtaining what they desire. Their use of prayer amounts to blasphemy. They certainly take the name of our holy God in vain. In the Middle Ages, as perhaps is still the case in certain parts of the world today, the superstition underlying such a view of prayer seems to have been quite prevalent. It cropped out particularly often in prayers addressed to the saints. To what lengths wickedness went in this respect and how absolutely certain people regarded prayer sent up to the saints as a magical trick which they might employ when it pleased them, is apparent from this story (perhaps a fictitious one), related by Erasmus and pointed to by Oliver Wendell Holmes (in the *Autocrat of the Breakfast Table*). Speaking of a storm at sea which had struck a vessel with terrific force and of the confusion, terror, and praying of the passengers, Erasmus said: "I could not help laughing to hear one fellow bawling out, so that he might be sure to be heard, a promise to St. Christopher of Paris — the monstrous statue in the great church there — that he would give him a wax taper as big as himself. 'Mind what you promise,' said an acquaintance who stood near him, poking him with his elbow;

'you could not pay for it if you sold all your things at auction.' 'Hold your tongue, you donkey!' said the fellow, but softly, so that Christopher should not hear him. 'Do you think I am in earnest? If I once get my foot on dry ground, catch me giving him so much as a tallow candle!' " One wonders whether the tribe of superstitious and very wicked people to which this man belonged has entirely died out.

Again, prayer must not be regarded as a substitute for work and proper use of one's mental faculties. The charge has been raised against Christians that instead of doing their duty in strenuous efforts when difficulties surround them, they fold their hands in prayer and let others exert themselves. Praying has been called a lazy man's method of meeting a crisis. Instead of toiling, these praying Christians, so it is said, want to obtain what they need by merely pressing the electric button of prayer, expecting that thereby all the forces of the universe will be put at their disposal. What a gross, unfair misrepresentation this is! It may be that here or there persons are found who think that, because they pray, they need not work. We all see how utterly such people misunderstand the meaning of prayer. They do not observe that Christ does not merely say, Pray that ye fall not into temptation, but, "Watch and pray." They have not sufficiently learned the stern rule laid down by St. Paul: "If any would not work, neither should he eat." They ought to consider that, when Peter says to Jesus that he and his companions had toiled all night and caught nothing, Jesus does not come to his aid by quickly filling the ship with fish, but by making him row out upon the lake and lower the net. Prayer is not a substitute for work, but it obtains the blessings of God upon our work. The true Christian prays, not to be spared all labor and perspiration, but to be spared the sad disappointment of plowing and sowing, hammering and building in vain. His slogan is, *"Ora et labora,"* Pray and work; not merely pray and not merely work. Both must be cultivated by us because that is what God has ordained.

XIX

Our prayer must be spoken in true faith, with full confidence in God's power and willingness to hear us; and in order that such confidence may dwell in us, we must ask according to His will. When we come to God with our petitions, one indispensable condition, if our prayer is to be God-pleasing, is that we have full trust in God's power and His readiness to hear us. Our Savior emphatically inculcates that truth. When He with one word had brought about the withering of the unfruitful, deceiving fig-tree and His disciples were amazed, He said to them: "Have faith in God; for verily I say unto you, That whosoever shall say unto this mountain, Be thou removed, and be thou cast into the sea, and shall not doubt in his heart, but shall believe that those things which he saith shall come to pass, he shall have whatsoever he saith. Therefore I say unto you, What things soever ye desire, when ye pray, believe that ye receive them, and ye shall have them," Mark 11, 22—24. The miracle that Jesus had performed was astounding. The words which He spoke to His disciples were not less so. Think of it. If you have faith in the power of God, Jesus says, you may by a mere word of prayer cast a huge mountain into the sea. The efficacy of prayer is unlimited, He tells us; but one condition must be fulfilled — the prayer must be spoken in true faith. There are several other passages where Christ uses words of the same import. Cf. Matt. 17, 20.

Before we consider what seems so startling in these words of Jesus, let us remind ourselves that Scripture in general prescribes a trusting, believing attitude of the heart for our prayers. When St. Paul urges Christians to pray, he says that they should lift up holy hands, without wrath and *doubting*, 1 Tim. 2, 8. St. James writes: "If any of you lack wisdom, let him ask of God, that giveth to every man liberally and upbraideth not, and it shall be given him. But let him ask in faith, nothing wavering. For he that wavereth is like a wave of the sea, driven with the wind and tossed. For let not that man think that he shall receive anything of the Lord," Jas. 1, 5—7. When a man had brought his son to Jesus and asked that the demon afflicting the child be expelled, the Savior said: "If thou canst believe; all things are possible to him that believeth," Mark 9, 23.

And is it not true that the very nature of prayer requires the presence of faith in those who approach God with requests? If a person doubts that God can and will hear his petition, then his prayer is merely a tempting of God and falls under the condemnation of the word "Thou shalt not tempt the Lord, thy God." Such a man says to himself, as it were: I am not sure that God can hear me and grant what I pray for. But I shall try; perhaps He can help me; we shall see. That is not true, childlike prayer. It is a frivolous playing and dallying with God's power and love.

It is presumptuous, an offense against the majesty of our great God. It means that the promises of God are trodden under foot and that instead of love and confidence toward God selfishness fills the heart of such a person. So, certainly, our prayers must be spoken in true faith.

But now we must approach the question which is asked frequently, Does Jesus actually say in the words spoken immediately after the withering of the fig-tree that every, every prayer of ours, if spoken in faith, will be heard? If He did say that, is it not too sweeping a word? Can it be true? Let us squarely face this question. About the meaning of the words of Jesus there can be no doubt. They are clear, and they are meant to be all-inclusive. Even so apparently impossible a thing as the removal, by mere prayer, of a large mountain like the Mount of Olives from its base into the sea can be accomplished, He says. The only condition He makes, as I said before, is that the prayer be offered in true faith. This condition contains the key to our problem. If we ask for miraculous things to happen, such a prayer will be effective if we pray fully believing that the prayer will be granted. But such a belief we can have only if we know we are praying for something that God intends to have done. The faith required cannot arise in us unless we have the assurance that our prayer is really in keeping with the will of God. "Can you really through prayer cast Mount Wilson into the Pacific Ocean?" somebody asks us. "Indeed we can," we reply. "Well, why don't you do it?" he says. We answer, "Why should we? If we knew that God wants us to pray for such a thing, we should pray for it with the full conviction that the miracle would come to pass. But there being no intimation from God that He expects us to pray for such a happening, we cannot offer that prayer with the assurance that it will be heard." In other words, we cannot fulfil the condition which Jesus mentions. The prayer of faith is not a freak prayer, asking God to perform all manner of strange, spectacular things; but it is a prayer which endeavors to conform entirely to God's will. Jesus says Luke 17, 6: "If ye had faith as a grain of mustard-seed, ye might say unto this sycamine tree, Be thou plucked up by the root and be thou planted into the sea, and it would obey you." "So you believe," somebody may say to me, "that by prayer you can take all the scrub-oaks in a park where they stand in thick clusters and plant them in the bald spots, where they might serve some good purpose?" "Certainly,"

I answer. "Why don't you do it and beautify our public breathing-places?" "I cannot offer such a prayer in true faith," is my reply, "because I have no information from God that He wants me to pray for such a thing."

This leads over to a discussion of an important Bible-passage bearing directly on this subject. 1 John 5, 14 the apostle tells us: "And this is the confidence that we have in Him, that, if we ask anything according to His will, He heareth us." And you might say this is a commentary on the passages we have been considering, in which Jesus has promised us fulfilment of every prayer which is spoken with full confidence. It answers the question for us when we can have full confidence as to the fulfilment of our petition. The reply is, When our prayer is according to God's will. If you have the assurance that God really wills a certain thing and expects you to pray for it, you may pray for it without the shadow of a doubt in your mind as to the granting of the petition, and it will be heard and fulfilled. When we ask ourselves, What are the things that fall into this category and are according to His will? the answer is, All spiritual blessings which we need for our soul's salvation. God has promised them to us, He is anxious to bestow them, and when we pray for them in true faith, they are actually given to us. He that prays, for instance, for a strong faith, not doubting that God hears his prayer, will certainly receive it. With respect to temporal blessings, as I pointed out before, we cannot pray with the same assurance except for the general conviction that God will do what is best for us. In such matters our vision is imperfect and defective and might overlook grave perils, and hence we cannot arrive at the full confidence that a certain thing we desire is absolutely the only good and proper boon for us under the circumstances. We know that it is God's will to bless us; but this very will of His may withhold from us the thing which we are asking for, because it would work harm to us if we received it. Shall we, to give an example, pray to God to grant us a long life? Most people desire longevity. But must we not say that a long life in some instances turns out to be a curse instead of a blessing and that for many people it would have been far better if they had died young, at a time when they were still Christians and were leading a godly life, while later on they fell into gross sins and disgrace and caused no end of heartaches to their friends and relatives and finally had to look upon themselves with loathing and disgust? Can you, then, say with absolute assurance that it is God's will that you should reach a very high age, and can you pray for it with the full confidence that it will be granted you? Can a Christian farmer, to take another instance, pray to God for a good crop with the full confidence that He will grant this particular petition? He will certainly pray to God for such a blessing; he should do it, and his friends should all join him in this prayer; but we must say that, since we do not know whether a good crop would really serve his highest interests, and since therefore we are not sure that it is God's will to grant him a good crop, such a prayer ought to be a conditional one, and the decision as to the fulfilment should be placed into the hand of God. God will, of course, hear your prayer for good crops if you plead in the right spirit; but He may hear it differently from the way you expect and at present desire it.

Somebody probably will say, If the great promises of Christ as to the efficacy of our prayers are hedged about with such limitations, what is the use of having them? What are they for? The reply is obvious. Through these promises Christ creates in us the conviction that our prayers are not in vain, that, on the contrary, they are a great force. He furthermore thereby encourages us to become diligent in prayer, gladly approaching the throne of God with our problems and requirements. Let me give you a homely illustration. You wish to assure your little boy that, if he asks for what he needs in the proper way, you will give it to him, and so you say, "Son, whatever you ask for, I will give you, provided it is good for you, even if it should be my whole farm." Your little boy may at once test that promise and say, "Father, let me have a thousand dollars." You will say, "No; I cannot give that money to you." "But you promised it," says the boy. "Yes," you reply, "but I added, If it is good for you. And the gift of a thousand dollars would not be good for you." "Well, why did you tell me that you would be willing to give me even the whole farm?" the little lad will continue his cross-examination. And you will answer, "My son, just to assure you that I take great delight in having you ask me for what you need and in supplying your needs when you come to me with your requests." Yes, Christ's promises have their purpose, and they are true, but they must not be misunderstood and misused.

In the biography of Charles Kingsley, the famous English author and preacher, written by his wife, we find some paragraphs that may well be quoted here (Charles Kingsley, *His Letters and Memories of His Life*, Vol. II, p. 112 ff.): "The summer of 1860 was a very wet one. Rain fell almost incessantly for three months. The farmers were frightened, and the clergy all over the country began to use the prayer against rain. Mr. Kingsley did not do so. The cholera had long been threatening England, and his knowledge of physical and sanitary science told him how beneficial this heavy rain was — a gift from God at that particular moment to ward off the enemy which was at hand, by cleansing drains, sweeping away refuse, and giving the poor an abundance of sweet, clean water. All this he explained to his own people by preaching them a sermon on Matt. 7, 9—11, which was published under the title of '*Why Should We Pray for Fair Weather?*' of which he thus speaks:

" 'A certain sermon of mine about the rains, which shocked the clergy of all denominations, pleased deeply, thank God, my own laborers and farmers. They first thanked me heartily for it and begged for copies of it. I then began to see (what I ought to have seen long before) that the belief in a good and just God is the foundation, if not of a scientific habit of mind, still of a habit of mind into which science can fall and seed and bring forth fruit in good ground.'

" 'How do we know,' he says in this sermon, 'that in praying God to take away these rains we are not asking Him to send the cholera in the year to come? I am of opinion that we are. I think, I have thought long, that one or two more dry summers, keeping the springs at their late low level, would have inevitably brought back the cholera or some other kind of pestilence. But even if that particular guess be wrong, this I believe, and this I will preach, that every drop of rain which is falling now is likely to be not a plague and a punishment but a blessing and 'a boon to England and to Englishmen.

" 'Now perhaps you may understand better why I said that I was afraid of being presumptuous in praying for fine weather. I do not blame any one for so doing; God forbid! Who am I to judge another? To his own master each man stands or falls. All I say is that, looking at the matter as I do, it would be presumptuous in me; and I do not wish to do it unless I am commanded by my bishop, in which case my duty is to obey orders. But I do shrink from praying for fine weather on my own responsibility.' " The hierarchical conception of the constitution of the Church reflected in the reference to the bishop we of course reject.

To a minister who had asked for further light Kingsley wrote: "I feel very deeply the difficulties which you put as corollaries from my sermon on the weather; nevertheless I can and do pray and hope that I always shall pray. I do not pretend to see my (logical) way clearly on this most subtle and important point; but this I see, that trials cannot be put into the same category as natural phenomena. Trials are part of our spiritual education, chastisements, to teach us somewhat; and if we learn the lesson beforehand, we may pray to have the sin forgiven and the chastisement remitted; and even if we have not, we can, and in effect do, cry out of the darkness to the boundless love of God by an instinct more rational and divine than all logic. And this may apply even to natural phenomena. To pray that there may not be a thunder-storm is to me presumptuous, because the thunder-storm will not come unless it is wanted. To pray that the particular lightning-flash may not strike my child is not presumptuous. It is only asking God that a peculiar combination of circumstances which will bring my child under the influence of the laws of electricity may not take place; and that God can and does arrange by a perpetual providence every circumstance whatsoever, so making laws take effect only when and where He chooses, I believe utterly. It may be answered, 'If it be right for the child to be struck, it will be; if not, not.' I know that — I believe that. Everybody does who is pious. Even those who believe in a quite magical effect from prayer will say, and rightly, when their prayers are not answered, 'It is God's will; it ought not to have been answered, therefore it was not.' All are driven to this; yet all pray and should pray. It is one of those paradoxes which no science can explain. All we can do is to eliminate from our prayers as much as we can all of self-will and selfishness and study and copy the Lord's Prayer, praying 'after that manner.' This is a poor answer; but if you be an honest man, you would sooner have an honest half-answer than a dishonest whole one."

XX

While we glory in the efficacy of prayer, we should not call it a means of grace. In Reformed circles it is quite common to call prayer a means of grace and to list it in the same group with the Word of God, Baptism, and the Lord's Supper. A brief word is required on that subject. It is evident at once that here we are dealing with a matter of terminology, and it would be wrong if we started a battle just because certain people use a term in a different sense from that in which we employ it, especially if the term does not occur in the Bible. That precisely is the case here; the expression "means of grace" is not found in the Holy Scriptures, but has been coined by the Church, and hence we should be careful before we declare hostilities against any one because of his use of it. When we define "means of grace" as the Lutheran Church does, prayer cannot be regarded as such a means. With us a means of grace is something in which God comes to us and assures us of His grace and bestows His Holy Spirit. The Gospel and the Sacraments are such means; God is there speaking to us and giving us gracious, loving assurances and conferring the Holy Spirit, the Comforter, whom He has promised. But in prayer the situation is different. There *we* are the ones that are acting; we approach God with praise and with our requests. It has been correctly stated that, while the means of grace are God's hand stretched out to us, prayer is the hand which we stretch out and up to God. Though we do not wish to deny that prayer is a source of great blessing to us and very emphatically declare it to be one of the greatest privileges and boons we enjoy, our terminology does not permit us to call it a means of grace.

XXI

Our Savior inculcates persistence in prayer. Our meditation on prayer would be incomplete if we did not say a word about the instruction which Jesus gave to His disciples on the blessedness of persistency in prayer. In several of His parables He dwelt on this very feature and earnestly admonished that it be cultivated. There is the parable of the person persistent in shameless begging, who at midnight arouses his friend and asks for bread because he has received hungry company and there is nothing to eat in his house, Luke 11. Then there is the parable of the Importunate Widow, who is harassed by an adversary and does not stop pleading with the unjust judge till he consents to help her, Luke 18, 1 ff. And besides we have the beautiful account of the Syrophenician woman and of her struggle with the Lord, showing how she, when Jesus was apparently unwilling to listen to her request, persisted and finally prevailed, Mark 7, 24 ff.

We see from this that our God is pleased with persevering,

continuing prayer; otherwise the Savior would not encourage us
to engage in it. We ourselves find it disgusting when a person,
after we have on good grounds refused his request, unceasingly
troubles us with it. We may finally like the unjust judge in the
parable, just to be rid of the tormenting petitioner, give him
what he desires, doing it with a sour, sullen expression on our
face. "What a pest you are! Have it your way!" we probably
exclaim. But our God is not displeased with such tactics. His
fatherly heart rejoices in being thus appealed to, even though in
His wisdom He cannot at once grant our requests. Matthew
Henry says: "We prevail with men by importunity because they
are displeased with it, but with God because He is pleased with it."

This subject apparently leads to a difficulty. What I have
just said about perseverance in prayer seems to be at variance with
what Jesus says Matt. 6, 7. 8: "But when ye pray, use not vain
repetitions, as the heathen do; for they think that they shall be
heard for their much speaking. Be not ye therefore like unto
them; for your Father knoweth what things ye have need of
before ye ask Him." Is that not the same as saying, Be not
importunate in your prayers, do not persist in making petitions,
since God knows very well what your needs are? The explanation
is that the heathen believed in quantity in prayer and repeated
their formulas, which often were meaningless, over and over again.
Such a thing is an abomination in the sight of God. But that
we approach God and pour out our heart to Him and keep
on doing this is something on which He looks with favor. Such
a course is proper for children who love their Father and who
have confidence in Him. A French theologian, Quesnel, seems
to have put the matter correctly when he said: "To pray always
and to speak but little is one of the paradoxes of the Gospel; this
duty requires little of the tongue, much of the heart. A man may
be justly said always to pray when he has God always present to
his mind and is always desiring Him." (Quoted in the *Study
Bible,* volume on St. Luke.) The gospels simply report these two
utterances of Jesus, and we have to let them both stand, the
prohibition to shout loud and long as if God were deaf and the
command to be urgent and unwearied in prayer. In addition to
what has been said by way of harmonization I might state that
the two passages treat not of the same matter, but of different
questions. One answers the question whether it requires many

words to make God hear and understand us; the other answers the question whether we should cease praying when God apparently refuses to grant our request.

So let us beware of the mere outward repetition of prayers such as we find in the Roman Catholic circles with their double-quick, rapid-fire recitations of the rosary and, on the other hand, of the skeptical, doubting, half-hearted praying which ceases when after a sentence or two the clouds are still there.

XXII

As to the use of the Lord's Prayer and other formal or printed prayers, the place of praying or posture in praying, and similar matters, whatever instruction the Bible offers us must be gratefully heeded, and no practise must be introduced which militates against the childlike approach of the Christian to his heavenly Father. Realizing that my space is limited, I am here trying to call attention briefly to a number of points which ought to receive attention. That we have a model prayer in the Lord's Prayer needs no proof, since it comes from Christ Himself. In asking, as it does, chiefly for spiritual blessings and in laying stress chiefly on the glory of God and of His kingdom, in the humility which it breathes and the conviction of absolute dependence on God, and in its avoidance of all superfluous phraseology, it points the way for our own prayers. Let us continue to use the Lord's Prayer joyfully, gratefully, but beware of making it a poor, tortured martyr by repeating it in a thoughtless, indifferent, mechanical fashion. Who of us can say that here he is not guilty?

That Jesus has given the Lord's Prayer to us disposes of a question which has often been asked, whether it is right to employ formal, printed prayers in our church services and private devotions. Jesus would not have given us a model prayer if such a thing were wrong. That in our circles, too, criticism is now and then voiced regarding the use of what has been called "canned prayers" and that this criticism is justified if the prayers are not read with becoming reverence and earnest devotion, is something we should not hide from ourselves.

To proceed, we note that in His Word God does not single out one place as the only one where prayers may be said. On the contrary, His apostle tells us that men should pray *everywhere,* 1 Tim. 2, 8. Accordingly we see that the children of God spoken of in the Bible prayed in the most varied localities, on mountaintops, in deserts, on ships, in caves, in the Temple, in their homes, and in other places. But we must not overlook that our Savior mentions one place as especially suitable because there we shall not incur the danger of making a display of our prayer, — it is the inner room, where we are unseen. "Thou, when thou prayest, enter into thy closet, and when thou hast shut thy door, pray to thy Father, which is in secret; and thy Father, which seeth in secret, will reward thee openly," Matt. 6, 6. Jesus spoke these words in opposition to the practise of the hypocrites of His day, who prayed standing in the synagogs and on the street corners to be seen. Such praying is offensive to God. It is not a speaking of the heart to God but a mere making of words intended to impress the spectators. If you catch yourself in such a sin, then repent and make the inner room, where you are all alone with your God, your favorite place of prayer. That our churches should be places of prayer for us we can see, for instance, from the New Testament description of the early Christian services.

As to our posture in praying, we have no specific command of God. We find that some of the saints prayed in a kneeling position, for instance, Daniel; others stood (so Hannah); David offered prayer at one time while he was sitting, 2 Sam. 7, 18; and St. Paul says: "I will therefore that men pray everywhere, *lifting up holy hands,* without wrath and doubting," 1 Tim. 2, 8. The lifting up of hands mentioned here is referred to elsewhere in the Scriptures also; cf. Ps. 141, 2. In our churches we like to pray with folded hands. On this subject Meusel's *Handlexikon* says: "Folding of the hands, an expression of trust and confidence in God, to whom, conscious of our own weakness, we surrender ourselves unconditionally, has accompanied prayer since most ancient times. Some liturgists likewise pointed out that, when the hands are folded, hands and fingers form the shape of a cross."

Special hours for prayer have the sanction of ancient Jewish usage: cf. Acts 3, 1. We all know that no particular time has been appointed for us. What is important is that we take time for prayer, realizing that the time of day is not essential. In order not to forget communing with God, it is advisable that we should have stated, fixed periods for ourselves when we pray before our heavenly Father. And withal, we must not forget that St. Paul exhorts us, "Pray without ceasing," 1 Thess. 5, 17. Our hearts should always be attuned to the presence of God and be conscious of His being always near us, ready to hear every sigh we may utter and to strengthen us as in weakness we turn to Him. When we adopt a schedule of prayer for ourselves, we must beware of course of falling into mere mechanical formalism, which is incompatible with the filial attitude of the heart toward God.

XXIII

Prayers spoken while a person is committing a mortal sin are not acceptable to God. The Scriptures several times issue warnings that we must not think God will hear our prayer if we are consciously, deliberately, serving sin. A mortal sin, it will be recalled, is a sin which one commits consciously, deliberately, and which destroys one's faith. Jesus makes mention of the unforgiving spirit as a barrier which rises between our prayers and God. He says in Mark 11, 25. 26, after He has exhorted His disciples to have faith in God and has given them the great promise that whatever they pray for in true faith will be given them: "And when ye stand praying, forgive if ye have aught against any that your Father also which is in heaven may forgive you your trespasses. But if ye do not forgive, neither will your Father which is in heaven forgive your trespasses." If a person has an unforgiving spirit, he is committing a mortal sin, a sin which kills his spiritual life. Jesus says, when such a man prays, God will not forgive his trespasses. This certainly implies that God will not hear the prayers of such a person. In Ps. 66, 18 we have the definite statement "If I regard iniquity in my heart, the Lord will not hear me," a statement which shows that serving iniquity on our part makes it impossible for God to grant our prayers. A similar statement we have in Job 27, 9: "Will God hear his cry [the cry of the hypocrite] when trouble cometh upon him?" The answer of course is, No. Such a person will cry in vain. The service of sin makes our praying a futile, vain attempt to reach the throne of the Lord. Whoever comes to the presence of God with a heart bent upon evil-doing falls under the condemnation of James, mentioned before, chap. 4, 3: "Ye ask and receive not because ye ask amiss, that ye may consume it upon your lusts."

How can it be otherwise? If a person is intent on transgressing the commandment of God and still turns to God in prayer, how can he expect to be given a favorable reception? He is flouting God's command and treading it under foot. If he still turns to God, it is not because he is God's child, but merely because he wishes to obtain some benefits. He poses as a friend of God, and at the same time he consciously opposes Him. Such hypocrisy will not deceive God. Praying in such a way reminds one of that German nobleman who, as the story goes, bought from John Tetzel an indulgence for a sin which he was intending to commit and who in one of the next nights robbed Tetzel of all the money he carried with him and who, when cursed by Tetzel, countered by producing the letter of indulgence which he had duly paid for. It served this monk right to be caught in his own trap. But if anybody thinks he can go on sinning and at the same time say his prayers and be heard, he will find that God is not mocked. St. Paul exhorts the Christians to whom he writes that they in their prayers should lift up *holy* hands, without wrath and doubting. Accordingly, let us see to it that our hands are not defiled by the filth of deliberate, conscious wrong-doing when we pray.

XXIV

Joint prayer is inculcated by God and given a special promise. We must not overlook that rejection of the Triune God and of Christ and persistent adherence to false teaching or to a sinful life form a barrier against joint prayer. When the apostle says Eph. 5, 18 ff.: "Be filled with the Spirit, speaking to yourselves in psalms and hymns and spiritual songs, singing and making melody in your heart to the Lord; giving thanks always for all things unto God and the Father in the name of our Lord Jesus Christ," He inculcates joint prayer. And what can there be more beautiful than this, that a number of God's children unite in going to the Throne of Grace with their petitions and their thanksgiving? That Jesus is well pleased with such an activity He has shown by His promise in Matt. 18, 19. 20, saying: "Again I say unto you, That, if two of you shall agree on earth as touching anything that they shall ask, it shall be done for them of My Father which is in heaven. For where two or three are gathered together in My name, there am I in the midst of them." Joint prayer is effective, Jesus says thereby. It can accomplish much. When several of you implore God for a blessing, He will certainly not turn a deaf ear to you. We should for that reason put a high valuation on our joint prayers in the church and in the family circle; and if there were no other reason for churchgoing, the consideration that there we pray together with our fellow-Christians should be a sufficient inducement for us to attend.

We must not forget, however, that joint prayer cannot be practised with anybody and everybody. We cannot pray with people who are not Christians at all, rejecting the doctrines of the Trinity and of Christ's redemption. They cannot pray; how, then, can we join them in prayer? I cannot pray with a Mohammedan. He addresses Allah, a fictitious god, in his prayers. There can be no united worship between him and me. The Jew refuses to pray to the Triune God; hence I cannot pray with him. The same thing is true of the Unitarian. Those with whom I am to pray must belong to the holy Christian Church, the communion of saints. All who are members of this Church, the so-called invisible Church, are united with each other by the unseen bond of faith in the divine Savior. Where there is no evidence of the existence of this unseen bond, there is no justification for prayer-fellowship. What we think of primarily when we here speak of evidence is of course the profession people make of their religious convictions, a profession the truthfulness and sincerity of which no one except the person making it and the omniscient God can in all cases determine.

It must next be said that even in the circle of those who call themselves Christians and profess belief in the Triune God we cannot at once and always pray with everybody. One recalls that St. Paul in a passage of overwhelming power tells the Corinthians that the name "brother" could not suffice to keep a person in their fellowship if he was addicted to the service of sin. "But now I have written unto you," he says, "not to keep company if any man that is called a brother be a fornicator, or covetous, or an idolater, or a railer, or a drunkard, or an extortioner; with such an one, no, not to eat," 1 Cor. 5, 11. The people that he points to were called members of the Church, disciples of Jesus Christ. And still the stern order goes forth not even to eat with them, which implies that much less the sweetness and comfort of Christian prayer-fellowship could be granted them. What they needed was not a little coddling and petting and coaxing, but a stern lesson, making them realize how completely they had cut themselves off from the body of Christ. This, then, may be our opening consideration as we ask ourselves whether we may grant the privilege of joint prayer with us to everybody who calls himself a Christian, that the name Christian displayed by a person cannot be considered a sufficient basis for me in establishing such a fellowship with him. Of course, as I asserted above, the person with whom I am to pray must hold membership in the Church of our divine Savior as far as I can see. With all believers I am united through an invisible bond in a fellowship which God Himself has established. No one else can offer a true prayer. What I endeavor to point out just now, however, is that the mere possession or presentation of the name Christian on the part of a person coming to me does not justify me in having joint prayer with him. There must be, to put it briefly, nothing either in his doctrine or in his life that makes it impossible for me to unite with him in going to the throne of God.

Let us begin viewing this matter by first examining what sort of life would hinder the establishment of prayer-fellowship between a person calling himself a Christian and us. That such a life is conceivable is plain enough from the words of St. Paul quoted before. He lays before us a catalog of sins every one of which should act as a barrier to fellowship: fornication, covetousness, that is, avarice or greed, idolatry, railing, that is, the abusing of other people's character, drunkenness, and extortion. Naturally St. Paul does not desire the Corinthians to look upon this list as exhaustive, but merely as indicating the kind of life or conduct which makes Christian fellowship impossible.

We are shown in the Scriptures, however, that even sins which are not of this gross, glaring type, if persisted in, erect a barrier between the Christian who is loyal to God's Word and his fellow congregation-member who is manifesting indifference. In the Christian circles of Thessalonica the notion had spread that the day of Judgment would appear very soon, and a number of people as a result gave themselves over to a disorderly life, refusing to work any longer and relying for their maintenance on the kindness of others. The apostle censures them in stern words, 2 Thess. 3, 6. 11. 14. 15: "Now, we command you, brethren, in the name of our Lord Jesus Christ that ye withdraw yourselves from every brother than walketh disorderly and not after the tradition which ye received of us. . . . For we hear that there are some which walk among you disorderly, working not at all but are busybodies. . . . And if any man obey not our word by this epistle, note that man and have no company with him that he may be ashamed. Yet count him not as an enemy but admonish him as a brother." The conduct of the people here criticized was reprehensible and brought disgrace upon the Christian name, but it did not at once destroy Christian faith; for St. Paul urges that they be admonished as brethren. But for the time that it lasted, their sin severed the ties of fellowship. We must conclude, then, that where people lead a life of sin and refuse to heed admonition, a barrier to prayer-fellowship is being erected, and before there can be joint prayer with them, this sinning has to cease. That there are cases of sinning where it is apparent that what would normally act as a barrier to prayer-fellowship is merely a weakness, which we must patiently bear with, and that in general an unbrotherly, unevangelical, legalistic procedure must be avoided should not be overlooked.

How sinful conduct erects a barrier to prayer-fellowship might be shown in a few examples. Let us think of one of our ministers going about on his errands of instruction and mercy in his parish. One day he notices a stranger sitting by the roadside who, sad to say, is beastly drunk. The next day this stranger comes to his house and wishes to have joint prayer with him. The pastor recognizes him at once as the man whom he saw in such a pitiful state the day before. The stranger says, "Surely you will pray with me, because I am a Christian and even a fellow-Lutheran." What will the pastor say? "Before we can have prayer together, I must speak to you of something I saw yesterday. You call yourself my brother, but you have erected a barrier between yourself and me by your drunkenness. Something will first have to be done about that barrier." Possibly the stranger will be able to explain his intoxicated condition as involving no moral fault on his part. But there can be no doubt about the existence of a hindrance to prayer-fellowship till the matter has been looked into and properly adjusted. Similarly in a congregation, if one of the members of the church becomes guilty of a mortal sin, it must be recognized that a barrier is being erected between that man and his fellow congregation-members; that, while prayer-fellowship will not cease at once, the sin will have to be repented of; otherwise the barrier will become complete and stand. Matt. 18, 15 ff. with its instruction on the course we should follow in dealing with a sinning brother brings this out clearly. That sins which are not faith-destroying in themselves will, if persisted in, make prayer-fellowship impossible has been shown above.

What I have just said of the destructive nature of a life of sin for prayer-fellowship is true likewise of adherence to false doctrine. Imagine that a man comes to one of our pastors and desires the benefits and consolations of prayer-fellowship with him, saying that he is a Christian. The pastor, while glad to hear such a request, will be mindful of what St. John says 1 John 4, 1: "Beloved, believe not every spirit but try the spirits whether they are of God, because many false prophets are gone out into the world." Thinking of these words, he cannot at once give the hand of brotherly fellowship to his visitor. He will have to ask him what doctrine he professes. Let us imagine that the stranger says: "I am a Methodist, and I know that you are a Lutheran; there are points of difference between us, but they do not amount to very much; we are both Christians, hence let us pray together." The Lutheran pastor would have to reply: "Listen, my friend. You reject some things that are very dear to me, things that I should be willing to give my life for, for instance, the real presence of Christ's body and blood in the Lord's Supper. There is a barrier between you and me which first will have to be looked at." Whether the two can ultimately have prayer-fellowship will depend on developments in the conversation.

That we are not going too far when we say that adherence to false doctrine is a barrier to prayer-fellowship is evident from the insistence with which Jesus has commanded that we remain faithful to everything that He has taught. When He said to His disciples Matt. 28, 20 that they were to teach people to observe all things whatsoever He had commanded them, He left no one in doubt as to what He considered the proper attitude toward His revelation. And again, when He says John 8, 31. 32: "If ye continue in My Word, then are ye My disciples indeed, and ye shall know the truth, and the truth shall make you free," we have conclusive evidence that loyalty to His Word is something that He inculcates. Whoever is not loyal to the words of Jesus, adding here, subtracting there, altering this or that teaching, is not so faithful to the Savior as he should be. His deviation from the teaching of Jesus may be unknown to him and not at all deliberate; perhaps merely the mind is leaving the right track and the heart is not rebelling; but being a deviation from what the divine authority has laid down, it is a serious offense, and we cannot ignore it. If Jesus had left the matter of strict adherence to His teachings to our own choice and preference, we could pursue a different course in this respect; but since He has plainly indicated His will, we have to acknowledge that he who leaves the pure, holy teachings of the Scriptures thereby builds a wall between himself and us. The startling words of warning uttered by St. John in Rev. 22, 18 f. concerning adding to, or subtracting from, the message he wrote must show every one that here we are not speaking of an insignificant little point.

The matter can be approached from another point of view, too. Whoever is altering the teachings of Jesus thereby is creating a division in the Church, placing himself in opposition to all who adhere to Christ's doctrine. We have been told by St. Paul that we must avoid such division-makers, Rom. 16, 17. That implies of course that we do not have prayer-fellowship with them. This same admonition holds with respect to those who are not the originators but the perpetuators of the divisions, carrying on the work of the captains of strife, discord, and disharmony by teaching the same errors as these men. A number of generations have passed between Roger Williams, who was one of the first to teach Baptist principles in what we now call the United States, and a present-day adherent of such principles, and the latter may be as peaceful and gentle a member of our race as you care to meet; still by perpetuating the false teachings of Roger Williams, he is helping to continue the division which these teachings have caused among those that bear the Christian name, and one cannot see how such a one can prove that we do not have to apply Rom. 16, 17 against him and say to him that, as long as he maintains such divisive principles, he is placing a barrier between himself and us, obstructing prayer-fellowship.

Probably somebody will say that we have every reason to believe that there are true children of God among those who are adherents of false doctrine and that, if we make such adherence a hindrance to prayer-fellowship, the inevitable result is that we deny the blessings of such fellowship to some people who are members of God's own family. This is true, we have to reply. It is something we regret but cannot alter. If we were omniscient, we should not find ourselves in this predicament. As it is, whenever a man comes to us with a false teaching on his lips or a sinful act in progress of being committed by his hands, we have the duty to make mention of these things and cannot establish prayer-fellowship with him as if there were no obstacles in the way. It may be that the obstacles can readily be removed; but their existence cannot *a priori* be ignored. The false teaching may not have affected the faith of the man in question at all; the sin which he commits may be an unconscious one; that must be granted. But we are not readers of men's hearts. We can merely judge by what we see and hear. In humility, with fear and trembling, we must do our duty and point to what is wrong, rebuking and reproving with all patience. (Cf. 2 Thess. 3, 6.) If we are filled with the Spirit of Christ, it will soon become apparent that what we are condemning in refusing prayer-fellowship to adherents of false teaching is not the person we are dealing with but violations of God's revelation which we observe and to which the majesty of God's Word compels us to draw attention. True love for my neighbor, too, dictates the course outlined. For it is undeniable that his recognition of the errors into which he has fallen is of greater importance to him than my prayer-fellowship.

I can here merely allude to the fact that prayer-fellowship with people bearing the Christian name but advocating erroneous teachings becomes impossible if thereby offense should be given or the truth denied. When offense is here spoken of, the term is used in the Biblical sense of making a brother stumble or leading him into sin. My praying with adherents of doctrinal errors may lead a person to think that strict loyalty to the Word of God is not at all required, and he may through my course and example become indifferent. In the strongest language possible the Lord warns us against any activity which might make a brother stumble spiritually. (Cf. Matt. 18, 6—9; Luke 17, 1 f.) Again, if my praying with those who are advocates of unscriptural teachings should involve a denial of the truth on my part, I certainly cannot engage in it, because disciples of Jesus must not deny, but confess their acceptance of, Him and His blessed teachings. To avoid being misunderstood, I ought to add that I here do not wish to pass judgment on the hundreds of cases where special circumstances obtain and a number of factors have to be considered before one can pronounce on the course that should be followed. What this discussion is concerned with is the laying down of general principles.

That such views as have been set forth just now are not found appealing in this unionistic, latitudinarian generation, where all insistence on purity of doctrine is anathema and wide laxity as to religious beliefs is considered a sign of good breeding, we ought not to consider surprising. It is the only kind of fruit that can be produced on a field where the soil, the fertilizer, and the seed itself are all gotten out of the valley of indifference. May God mercifully keep us from blowing the horn at which millions of mouths are nowadays exercising themselves, whose one melody is "Religious beliefs do not matter; one is as good as the other."

Thus we have now come to the end of our study. There still remains much to be said on the subject of Christian prayer. In fact, the longer one occupies oneself with it, the more one sees how inexhaustible it is. Can we do more in this life than make a beginning of the proper contemplation of this great topic which in the life to come we shall not only understand in theory, being furnished the key to its perplexing questions, but which we then shall perfectly understand in practise, too, our occupation as the cycles of eternity roll on being praise and thanksgiving before the throne of God and the Lamb? Let our prayer, then, be that through God's grace we may reach that realm of absolute understanding, of purity, and of perfection in prayer described by St. John in Rev. 7, 9—12: "After this I beheld, and, lo, a great multitude, which no man could number, of all nations, and kindreds, and people, and tongues, stood before the throne and before the Lamb, clothed with white robes and palms in their hands; and cried with a loud voice, saying, Salvation to our God, which sitteth upon the throne, and unto the Lamb. And all the angels stood round about the throne and about the elders and the four beasts and fell before the throne on their faces and worshiped God, saying, Amen: Blessing, and glory, and wisdom, and thanksgiving, and honor, and power, and might be unto our God forever and ever. Amen."

www.ingramcontent.com/pod-product-compliance
Lightning Source LLC
Chambersburg PA
CBHW031225090426
42740CB00007B/711